KU-191-464

ROBERT BURNS

The Kilmarnock Poems

(Poems, Chiefly in the Scottish Dialect, 1786)

Edited, with an introduction and notes, by
DONALD A. LOW
Reader in English Studies, University of Stirling

Dent: London and Melbourne
EVERYMAN'S LIBRARY

© Introduction, notes and editing, J. M. Dent & Sons Ltd, 1985
All rights reserved

Phototypeset in 9/12pt Trump Mediaeval by
The Word Factory Ltd., Rossendale, Lancs.
Made and printed in Great Britain by
Richard Clay (The Chaucer Press) plc, Bungay, for
J. M. Dent & Sons Ltd
Aldine House, 33 Welbeck Street, London W1M 8LX
This edition first published in Everyman's Library 1985

This book if bound as a paperback is
subject to the condition that it may
not be issued on loan or otherwise
except in its original binding

British Library Cataloguing in Publication Data
Burns, Robert, *1759–1796*
   The Kilmarnock poems.
   I. Title   II. Low, Donald A.
   821'.6   PR4312.K/

   ISBN 0–460–00343–7
   ISBN 0–460–01343–2

Contents

Preface

What is the unique communicative quality in the genius of Burns which has helped to make his work truly international? The publication at Kilmarnock in 1786 of *Poems, Chiefly in the Scottish Dialect* clearly stands as one of the decisive events in post-mediaeval Scottish literature. Beyond this, though, Burn's poetic fame has gone round the world, so that he is virtually on his own among major poets of the British Isles in being genuinely popular not only throughout Europe and North America, but also in Australasia, in the Soviet Union, and in Japan and the Orient. To date, his poetry has been translated into more than twenty languages.

The present edition of the volume of poems which made Burns famous is true to the original 1786 text, and is the first to be published incorporating both detailed marginal glossing and notes. It seeks to meet an obvious modern need, created by lack of familiarity with eighteenth-century Lowland Scots. My first aim has been to share the pleasure I find in Burns by making it possible for any reader to understand at a glance the literal meaning of the words on the page. (As an alternative or additional resouree, the glossary which the poet published with his work in 1786 is reproduced in full in Appendix A.) In my introduction, headnotes to individual poems, and notes, I have tried to provide clear and accurate guidance on some of the many points – biographical, historical, and literary – raised by an endlessly challenging and delightful collection of poems. A Select Bibliography lists further sources of information about Burns and his poetry.

In common with everyone who has worked on Burns during the past seventeen years, I owe a large debt to the editorial labours of the late James Kinsley in *The Poems and Songs of Robert Burns* (3 vols., Oxford, 1968). It is a pleasure for me to acknowledge indebtedness to the scholarship of G. Ross Roy in his revision and expansion of the standard edition of *The Letters of Robert Burns* (2 vols., Oxford, 1985).

The award of sabbatical leave in the spring semester of 1984 has enabled me to complete this edition, work on which has been helped in a variety of ways by the support of the University of Stirling and its Robert Burns Project. My warm thanks for their interest are due to Sir Kenneth Alexander, Principal and Vice-Chancellor of the University; to Mr R. G. Bomont, University Secretary; to Professors T. A. Dunn and A. N. Jeffares of the Department of English Studies; and to our Honorary colleagues, Professor David Daiches and Miss Jean Redpath. The responsibility for errors of fact or interpretation in these pages is of course mine alone.

It was an unforgettable privilege to enjoy the friendship of the late Dr R. S. Gilchrist of Edinburgh, sponsor of the continuing Burns Project at Stirling University. I am only sorry that he did not live to see in its new form a book of poems he loved and wanted to make accessible to all.

Mr W. A. Anderson, Honorary Secretary of the Burns Federation, has very kindly allowed me to make use of a card index to the *Burns Chronicle* (1892 –   ), prepared by his predecessor, the late Mr J. F. T. Thomson; while Mr William Cowan, Honorary Secretary of Irvine Burns Club, has made it easy for me to consult original Burns manuscripts at Irvine used as printer's copy in 1786. For other acts of kindness, I wish to record my gratitude to all those, too numerous to name, who have assisted my research in the British Library, the National Library of Scotland, the Mitchell Library, Glasgow, Stirling University Library (especially Douglas Mack), the Dick Institute, Kilmarnock, and the Burns Cottage Museum, Alloway.

I particularly wish to thank Tina Stewart, of Fortronic Information Systems (Edinburgh), for helping to convert my instinctive enthusiasm for Wang word-processing into practical knowledge; Tony Hewitt and his colleagues in Stirling University's very lively Computer Unit; and – not for the first time – Jocelyn Burton of J. M. Dent, the most helpful and dependable of editors.

No words can adequately sum up what I once again owe in this book to my wife Sheona for her unstinting encouragement, totally positive outlook, and sense of fun. To her, and to Chris and Kirsty, this edition is dedicated.

Chronology

1759   Robert Burns born at Alloway, near Ayr, 25 January.

1766   Burn's father becomes tenant of Mount Oliphant, a farm near Alloway.

1774   Burns writes his first song at harvest-time, to please Nelly Kilpatrick. 'Thus with me began Love and Poesy'.

1777   The family move to Lochlea Farm, by Tarbolton.

1780   Burns is active in founding a Bachelors' Debating Club at Tarbolton.

1784   His father dies at Lochlea. Burns and his brother Gilbert move to Mossgiel Farm, near Mauchline, leased from Gavin Hamilton.
Reads Fergusson's *Poems*.

1785   Meets Jean Armour, begins to 'puzzle Calvinism with . . . heat and indiscretion', and writes much poetry.

1786   Runs into trouble with Jean Armour's family, vainly tries to forget her in 'all kinds of dissipation and riot', parts from 'Highland Mary', and makes plans to emigrate to Jamaica. POEMS, CHIEFLY IN THE SCOTTISH DIALECT, published at Kilmarnock (late July). Burns gives up the idea of emigration, and goes to Edinburgh (November).

1787   First Edinburgh and London editions of *Poems*. Tours the Borders and the Highlands of Scotland, begins to contribute songs to James Johnson's *Scots Musical Museum*, and meets Mrs Agnes McLehose ('Clarinda').

1787–8   Much of this winter spent in Edinburgh.

1788   Burns acknowledges Jean Armour as his wife ('and so farewell Rakery!'), leases the farm of Ellisland, near Dumfries, and is commissioned as an exciseman. From now on, writes more songs than poems.

1789   Begins work in the Excise at a salary of £50 per annum.
        Blake, *Songs of Innocence*.
1790   Writes 'Tam o' Shanter'.
1791   Gives up Ellisland in favour of full-time excise work, and
        moves to Dumfries. On a visit to Edinburgh, says farewell
        to Clarinda.
1792   Burns is asked to contribute songs to George Thomson's *A
        Select Collection of Original Scotish Airs* (1793–1818). He
        is accused of political disaffection. This charge blows over,
        but 'I have set, henceforth, a seal on my lips, as to these
        unlucky politics.'
1793   Second Edinburgh edition of *Poems* and first set of
        Thomson's *Select Collection* published.
1794   Appointed Acting Supervisor of Excise.
        Blake, *Songs of Experience*.
1795   Joins in organizing Dumfries Volunteers. Severely ill with
        rheumatic fever.
1796   Burns dies at Dumfries, 21 July.
1798   Wordsworth and Coleridge, *Lyrical Ballads*.

Introduction

When he published *Poems, Chiefly in the Scottish Dialect* at Kilmarnock at the end of July 1786, twenty-seven-year-old Robert Burns believed that he was about to emigrate. Bringing out a book of poems was at once a bid for poetic fame, a poet's farewell to his native Scotland, and an attempt to raise a little cash. Burns's life was in a tangle. There was a spirit of defiance – and more than a hint of desperation – about his frame of mind in the period immediately before and after publication.

Burns's father had died in February 1784, worn out by the struggle to make a living for his family as a tenant farmer in central Ayrshire. Shortly afterwards, Burns and his brother Gilbert took a lease on the farm of Mossgiel, near Mauchline: but poor soil, bad harvests and lack of capital were all against their success. Later, Burns was to comment, 'I entered on this farm with a full resoluton, "Come, go to, I will be wise!" – I read farming books; I calculated crops; I attended markets . . . but the first year from unfortunately buying in bad seed, the second from a lean harvest, we lost half of both our crops; this overset all my wisdom . . .'[1] Then in the spring of 1786 the breaking of his relationship with a local girl made the future seem bleak. Briefly, Burns had wooed and made pregnant Jean Armour, a girl from his own village of Mauchline. The couple wanted to wed, and Burns went so far as to give Jean a document promising marriage (or possibly stating that it had taken place) – which would have been sufficient evidence of their new status in the eyes of the community. But Jean Armour's parents objected to her having anything to do with, let alone marrying, a penniless farmer whose reputation was that of rake and tearaway. The document was destroyed, and Jean was sent away to Paisley and forbidden to have anything more to do with Burns. The episode drove the poet, in his own words, 'into all kinds of dissipation and riot'.

Given this situation of wounded love and pride over Jean Armour, and continuing poverty, it is hardly surprising that Burns should have responded positively – if less than eagerly – to the news that an estate at Port Antonio on Jamaica (owned by a Scotsman from Ayr) was looking for an Assistant Overseer, or Book-keeper. He accepted the suggestion of his friend and landlord, Gavin Hamilton, that the publication of his poems by subscription would help to raise money towards the costs of emigration. In an autobiographical letter to Dr John Moore written in August 1787 Burns explained what his feelings were when he decided on publication:

> Before leaving my native country for ever, I resolved to publish my Poems. – I weighed my productions as impartially as in my power: I thought they had merit; and 'twas a delicious idea that I would be called a clever fellow, even though it should never reach my ears a poor Negro-driver, or perhaps a victim to that inhospitable clime gone to the world of Spirits . . . I was pretty sure my Poems would meet with some applause; but at the worst, the roar of the Atlantic would deafen the voice of Censure, and the novelty of west-Indian scenes make me forget Neglect.[2]

In the event, the extremely favourable reception given to his *Poems* made Burns opt to stay in Scotland. The special pressures of the spring and summer of 1786, which played so large a part in making him take his work to the Kilmarnock printer, gradually receded.

It may be added that Burns had at least toyed with the idea of publication for some time before the Armour crisis decided him on this course. According to his brother Gilbert, he considered publishing his 'Epistle to Davie' immediately after writing it:

> It was, I think, in the summer of 1784 . . . that he repeated to me the principal part of this epistle. I believe the first idea of Robert's becoming an author was started on this occasion. I was much pleased with the epistle and said to him I was of opinion it would bear being printed and that it would be well received by people of taste . . . Robert seemed very well pleased with my

criticism, and we talked of sending it to some magazine;
but as this idea afforded no opportunity of learning how
it would take, the idea was dropped.[3]

The first direct reference by the poet himself to the idea of giving his
poems the permanence of print is in the 'Epistle to James Smith',
written probably in early 1786:

> This while my notion's taen a sklent,
> To try my fate in guid, black *prent*;
> But still the mair I'm that way bent,
>   Something cries, 'Hoolie!
> .'I red you, honest man, tak tent!
>   Ye'll shaw your folly.

Burns's Most Prolific Phase as a Poet

Such was the range and overall excellence of Burns's poetic output
during 1785–6 that it was entirely reasonable that he should think of
publishing his poems. It has been noted that '1785–6 was as much an
annus mirabilis in his career as 1797–8 was in Wordsworth's'.[4]
There were two principal reasons for Burns's surge of creativity at
this time. The first lay in his reading of the brilliantly handled
Scottish poems of Robert Fergusson (1750–74). 'Rhyme,' Burns later
explained, 'except some religious pieces which are in print, I had
given up; but meeting with Fergusson's Scotch Poems, I strung my
wildly-sounding rustic lyre with emulating vigour.'[5] He used an
edition of Fergusson's poems published in 1782; and the evidence of
various references in his writings and also of poems showing the
influence of his 'elder brother in the Muse', points to his having
made this crucial discovery not earlier than 1784.

Essentially, what Fergusson offered him was a challenge.
Fergusson had died tragically young. As Burns saw it, such an ex-
ample must not be allowed to lapse. Burns was by instinct and by
choice a social poet, quick to catch the rhythms of living speech, and
strongly interested in describing the way of life and the values of
country-dwelling people who shared his background of experience –
an art which he called 'manners-painting'. He found in such poems

as Fergusson's 'Leith Races' and 'The Farmer's Ingle' at once a model and a point of departure, acutely observed socio-descriptive poetry with the potential for being developed further in Burns's hands towards full-blooded satire or explicit celebration.

A second motivating factor was psychological. It seems clear that, following the loss of a strict, respected father, Burns felt a compelling need to come to terms with complex and intense feelings, both of personal liberation, and of remorse at his own sometimes undisciplined conduct. His letters and first Commonplace Book allow us to glimpse a process of adjustment which took place over many months. As a result of this period of inner stock-taking, much of the poetry which Burns wrote during 1785 and 1786 has a new and confident note of authority, that of lived experience. He followed a sure artistic instinct in expressing with extraordinary candour and energy his hard-earned new awareness of his personal and social identity.

Omissions

During his most prolific phase, Burns wrote a number of fine poems which did not find their way into print in 1786. 'Holy Willie's Prayer' is an outstandingly successful verse satire on a named individual, a Mauchline church elder. 'Address to the Unco Guid, or the Rigidly Righteous' and 'The Ordination' are two other examples – the first deftly generalized, the second full of parish particulars – of poems inspired by ecclesiastical attitudes which Burns judged illiberal and worthy of ridicule. Local church affairs offered many subjects for satire; but when it came to selecting poems for publication, he was guided at least to some degree by an instinct for caution. Burns felt that he had gone through trouble enough for his sexual indiscretions, from Kirk Session and James Armour, without risking the loss through legal prosecution of whatever profit his book might bring him. Although in 1787 he was to add to his *Poems* 'Address to the Unco Guid' and 'The Ordination', he did not even then risk publishing 'Holy Willie's Prayer'.

In making his choice for publication, he omitted also all but a handful of the more than thirty songs he had written to pre-existent tunes, including those in a lively low-life cantata, 'Love and Liberty' (often known as 'The Jolly Beggars'). It seems likely that one or two of the songs which eventually found their way into the volume were chosen in some haste – like another category, the epigrams – mainly to increase its length. Excellent individual songs such as, for example, 'Mary Morison', would have added to the appeal of the whole, as 'Corn Rigs' undoubtedly does, but it has to be kept in mind that Burns's aim in 1786 was to provide a volume of *poems*: in that sense, literary convention pointed him in a different direction from his lifelong love of song. As regards 'Love and Liberty', it is of interest that when Burns submitted the manuscript of the cantata to a leading Scottish critic with a view to publishing it in the 1787 edition, the critic in question, Hugh Blair, a Church of Scotland divine, advised against inclusion on the grounds that what the poet had written was 'by much too licentious' to print. Burns then abandoned the idea of bringing before the public this particular work, a masterpiece.

Publication and Reception

In choosing to publish his poems by subscription, Burns followed a common eighteenth-century practice. In this way, an author could take steps in advance to cover himself against loss. John Wilson, printer in Kilmarnock, was the same age as Burns'.[6] He agreed to handle the printing, the responsibility to secure subscribers remaining the poet's own. In mid-April, Burns circulated *Proposals* for publishing by subscription, at three shillings, a stitched octavo volume, *Scotch Poems by Robert Burns*.[7] The *Proposals* – according to which the author had 'not the most distant *mercenary* view in Publishing' – were then vigorously passed about by Burns and by his friends. At this stage, certain individuals were notably successful in helping him. Gavin Hamilton, for instance, obtained the names of forty subscribers, Gilbert Burns seventy, and Robert Aiken, dedicatee of 'The Cotter's Saturday Night', no fewer than a hundred and forty-five names.

Printing of the collection, now entitled *Poems, Chiefly in the Scottish Dialect*, began on about 13 July. Three hundred and fifty people in Ayrshire and neighbouring districts had subscribed in advance for the book when, in an edition of six hundred and twelve copies, it appeared towards the end of the month. Its impact within the region was immediate and dramatic. Burns's first biographer, Robert Heron, describes it in this way:

> Old and young, high and low, grave and gay, learned or ignorant, all were alike delighted, agitated, transported. I was at that time resident in Galloway, contiguous to Ayrshire; and I can well remember, how that even the plough-boys and maid-servants would have gladly bestowed the wages which they earned the most hardly, and which they wanted to purchase the necessary clothing ... (On a Saturday evening) I opened the volume, by accident, while I was undressing, to go to bed. I closed it not, till a late hour on the rising Sunday morn, after I had read over every syllable it contained.[8]

By 28 August the printer had no more than thirteen copies of the book on his hands, unsold. In the autumn, Burns offered Wilson a second edition. Wilson declined, probably judging that there might be only a limited further sale in the Kilmarnock area. Any disappointment Burns felt at the close of their business relationship did not last long. Wilson and he had served each other well, in professional terms. Burns cleared, by his own statement, twenty pounds from the sale of the Kilmarnock edition.[9] Soon, his thoughts were centred on publishing, without Wilson's help, a new expanded edition of *Poems, Chiefly in the Scottish Dialect*; and this duly appeared in Edinburgh in April 1787. (See Appendix B.)

Comparison with other books printed by Wilson shows that Burns succeeded in eliciting a higher standard of printing lay-out than Wilson's usual. The poet took an active interest throughout: such features as the bold, clear handling of his text, and the consistent use of italics to mark rhetorical emphasis, point to his close involvement. Even more obvious evidence of Burns's determination to reach out to and communicate with his readers is provided by his carefully written Preface, well judged arrangement of the sequence of poems, and helpful Glossary of Lowland Scots. (Burns's Preface and Glossary are reproduced in Appendix A.)

Before long, Burns's work was being enthusiastically spoken of in Edinburgh. A chance incident which helped to make him decide to stay in Scotland took place a few weeks after publication. Dr George Lawrie, minister of Loudoun in Ayrshire, had sent a copy of the *Poems* to Dr Thomas Blacklock, a much respected blind poet from Ayrshire living in the capital. On 4 September, Blacklock wrote in glowing terms about the work:

> There is a pathos and delicacy in his serious poems; a vein of wit and humour in those of a more festive turn, which cannot be too much admired, nor too warmly approved; and I think I shall never open the book without feeling my astonishment renewed and increased . . .

He would see to it that the book reached the hands of Hugh Blair, the critic, and he added,

> It were . . . much to be wished, for the sake of the young man, that a second edition, more numerous than the former, could immediately be printed; as it appears certain that its intrinsic merit, and the exertions of the author's friends, might give it a more universal circulation than any thing of the kind which has been published within my memory.[10]

This letter was sent by Lawrie to Gavin Hamilton, who showed it to Burns. The latter's autobiographical letter to Dr John Moore, written in August 1787, shows with what excitement he reacted to Blacklock's praise:

> I had taken the last farewell of my few friends; my chest was on the road to Greenock; I had composed my last song I should ever measure in Caledonia, 'The gloomy night is gathering fast', when a letter from Dr Blacklock to a friend of mine overthrew all my schemes by rousing my poetic ambition. – The Doctor belonged to a set of Critics for whose applause I had not even dared to hope. – His idea that I would meet with every encouragement

for a second edition fired me so much that away I posted
to Edinburgh without a single acquaintance in town, or a
single letter of introduction in my pocket.[11]

Reviews of the Kilmarnock edition began to appear in October 1786.
In the eyes of James Sibbald's *Edinburgh Magazine*, Burns was 'a
striking example of native genius bursting through the obscurity of
poverty and the obstructions of a laborious life'. In December there
appeared in *The Lounger*, also published in Edinburgh, a long essay
in praise of Burns which was to prove influential far beyond Scot-
land. Its anonymous author, Henry Mackenzie – whose novel *The
Man of Feeling* Burns prized 'next to the Bible' – described the poet
in a memorable phrase as 'this Heaven-taught ploughman'.[12] The
implication that Burns owed everything to inspiration, and nothing
to familiarity with earlier Scottish and English poetry, was mis-
leading, but in terms of public relations Mackenzie's way of paying
tribute to his achievement proved triumphantly successful.
Edinburgh took up the ploughman poet as if he were her own; and
Burns was well and truly launched on the way to fame. Within a few
months, his poetry was being eagerly read in England by William
Cowper, who wrote to Samuel Rose on 27 August 1787,

> Poor Burns loses much of his deserved praise in this
> country through our ignorance of his language. I despair
> of meeting with any Englishman who will take the pains
> that I have taken to understand him. His candle is bright,
> but shut up in a dark lantern. I lent him to a very
> sensible neighbour of mine; but his uncouth dialect
> spoiled all; and before he had half read him through he
> was quite *ram-feezled* (exhausted).

Then in December 1787, Dorothy Wordsworth wrote to Jane Pollard
that her brother William had recommended the Kilmarnock edition
to her: 'he had read it and admired many of the pieces very much'.

Language and Style

If Cowper had a point in 1787, it is much more urgent two hundred years later that Burns's poems be accompanied by the kind of glossing which is easy to take in at a glance. Hence the translations of Scots words as they occur in this, the first separately published modern edition (as distinct from facsimile) of the Kilmarnock poems to have appeared. Burns himself wrote about wishing to publish his work while ever-changing language and manners allowed his meaning to be understood. Significantly, he included in the 1787 Edinburgh edition of his *Poems* an enlarged Glossary; he knew that even among his fellow-Scots some readers would otherwise be unable to make complete sense of the poems in Lowland Scots. Today, almost all readers, non-Scots and Scots alike, need even quite basic information, so rapid and continuous has been the decline in knowledge of the Lowland Scots tongue.[13]

Burns is at his best as a poet in Scots, simply because it was the language he spoke and heard every day of his life. Originally, Scots and northern English were variant forms of the same language. Never native to the Highlands, where Gaelic was spoken, Scots became firmly established in Lowland Scotland. As used by the poets of the late Middle Ages and early Renaissance, Dunbar, Henryson and Lyndsay, it is a flexible and copious literary language, drawing on a long tradition of spoken language development. The choice, by the Scottish Reformers, of English as the language of religious usage, the Union of the Crowns in 1603, and the Union of Parliaments in 1707, all had the effect of reducing the status of Scots, which in time gradually ceased to be a complete national language. Already by Burns's age – despite a brave attempt at literary revival by Allan Ramsay in the early eighteenth century – the Scots language was appreciably less rich or 'dense' in vocabulary and idiom than it had been in centuries past, and the process had begun of progressive fragmentation into a variety of dialects.

Belonging as he did, however, to an ancient and proud country district, Burns had the advantage of growing up with a relatively strong linguistic inheritance. It probably helped him in his assimilation and discovery over the years of the varied possibilities open to a poet using Scots that while his mother was a native Ayrshire woman, with a stock of songs and proverbial sayings, his father was an incomer from another notably well endowed linguistic area, the north-east of Scotland; and one moreover who insisted that his family acquire skills in the reading and writing of English. As a poet, Burns became confident and fluent in English, although as Scott noted 'he never seems to have been completely at his ease when he had not the power of descending at pleasure into that which was familiar to his ear, and to his habits'. In Scots he is totally at home, enriching the spoken dialect of Ayrshire with a judicious selection of words drawn from other sources, including his reading of Ramsay, Fergusson, and older Scottish poets. He does not need to strain after effect through any parade either of inkhorn terms or of local words, but instead is guided by what is appropriate in specific contexts. The lexical level varies in particular poems according to what Burns wishes to express. One poem which makes exceptionally interesting use of words and phrases he associated specifically with Ayrshire farmers of the older generation is 'The Auld Farmer's New-Year-Morning Salutation to His Auld Mare, Maggie'. 'Halloween' is an unusually and consciously difficult poem, in terms of vocabulary, because the poet has an antiquarian purpose and is deliberately recording as many local superstitions as he can; whereas 'To a Louse' is obviously much closer to the kind of Scots conversational idiom likely to have been understood anywhere in Scotland in 1786.

The poem which opens the collection offers immediate evidence of Burns's assurance and poise in handling language. Like many of his poems – the best-known example of all is 'Tam o' Shanter' – 'The Twa Dogs' is a poem for the speaking voice. Burns derives his mastery of pitch and timing from long practice not only in writing verse, but in listening to his countrymen speak: a finely tuned ear for Lowland Scots in combination with Scottish English enables him to capture the rhythms and idiom of actual spoken usage. Here are the first twelve lines:

'Twas in that place o' Scotland's isle,
That bears the name o' Auld King Coil,
Upon a bonie day in June,
When wearing thro' the afternoon,
Twa Dogs, that were na thrang at hame,
Forgather'd ance upon a time.

The first I'll name, they ca'd him *Caesar*,
Was keepit for his Honor's pleasure;
His hair, his size, his mouth, his lugs,
Shew'd he was nane o' Scotland's dogs,
But whalpit some place far abroad,
Whare sailors gang to fish for Cod.

Interestingly, the only Scots words – as distinct from the Scots forms 'na', 'hame', and 'ance' – which are used in the first verse paragraph are two adjectives, the widely known 'bonie' (lovely, attractive), and 'thrang' (busy, occupied). Yet, such is the significance of a distintive form of pronunciation, allied to the opening reference to Scotland, that the six lines are unmistakably the work of a native Scots poet. ('Auld King Coil', in line 2, is an eighteenth-century Ayrshire insider's way of denoting Kyle, the district where the poet was born.) Burns's exceptionally accurate sense of verbal phrasing is in operation throughout. For example, at the end of the single-sentence paragraph there is a slight quickening and then a slowing up, as casual description ('that were na thrang') is followed by deliberate emphasis ('Forgather'd ance'). It is one of the characteristic signs of the poet's control of his diction that 'ance upon a time' is spoken with a tiny but noticeable stress on 'ance', followed by a pause and then by the throwaway 'upon a time'. Substitute 'once upon a time' and the effect of the last line is lost.

Possibly the best single piece of advice for anyone coming to Scots poetry for the first time is to try reading the words aloud. Burns is writing about 'twa dogs'. The correct way to pronounce the noun is shown by the rhyme with 'lugs' (ears). In the preceding couplet, the rhyme gives another clue to pronunciation – 'pleasure' has a long ee sound. Here the vital information 'they ca'd him Caesar' is presented as it might be in real-life conversation, casually and almost as an afterthought. However, Burns also manages to convey through the matter-of-fact sounding collocation 'they ca'd him Caesar' a very Scottish recognition of the fact that 'Caesar' is no usual name for a dog in this society. There is already a hint, in 'Caesar . . . keepit for his Honor's pleasure', of the reductive power which lies ahead in 'The Twa Dogs'. What a grand name and style of life, the poet implies! He then makes a point of mentioning that Caesar has been 'whalpit' (whelped or born) across the Atlantic, 'Whare sailors gang to fish for Cod' – another deliberate touch of down-to-earth realism, reinforcing the reader's sense of an outlook on life which rejects all mere affectation.

As the poem develops, its language offers many individual clues to what could be called its incremental social meaning, like those mentioned above. Through his sure and varied knowledge of idiom, Burns works cumulatively to build up a strong and entirely distinctive poetic viewpoint on the action, often by creating unexpected groups of words drawn from different speech registers and placed together with ironic effect. It quickly becomes clear that Caesar is wise, friendly, and completely unsnobbish (such are not necessarily the attributes of his owner the laird or landowner). He may have begun life as 'nane o' Scotland's dogs', and now he belongs to a member of the gentry; but for all his exotic and aristocratic background, thanks to his naturally sociable attitude he is thoroughly at home in all the usual meeting-places of men and dogs, 'at kirk or market, mill or smiddie', and at once shows himself ready to spend the afternoon on equal terms with a 'ploughman's collie'. Caesar, in other words, is noble in nature as well as in name, an emperor indeed among dogs through his canine magnanimity. Luath – and Burns's implied readers – listen to what he has to say, therefore, with affection and respect.

The contents of the 1786 volume admirably represent both in scope and in quality the poetry Burns had written by this date. Strongly original satire can be seen at many points: it is to the fore in the genial dialogue between Caesar and Luath, in 'The Holy Fair', a rollicking – and for that very reason, devastating – exposé of hypocrisy in action at a typical Ayrshire convention, and in the disrespectful stance towards inherited religious taboo which Burns adopts in the 'Address to the Deil':

> An' now, auld *Cloots*, I ken ye're thinkan,
> A certain *Bardie's* rantin, drinkin,
> Some luckless hour will send him linkan,
>   To your black pit;
> But faith! he'll turn a corner jinkan,
>   An' cheat you yet.

Burns's 'manner-painting' strain, about which he writes in 'The Vision', is seen in 'The Cotter's Saturday Night', an essentially realistic if also idealized picture of family life among the rural poor (which at once established itself as a popular favourite on publication), and in 'Halloween', where he supplies a detailed narrative account of particular local customs and superstitions. Poems such as 'The Auld Farmer's New-Year-Morning Salutation to His Auld Mare, Maggie' and 'To a Mouse, on Turning Her up in Her Nest, with the Plough', show the generous, swiftly inclusive sympathy of someone who understands that animals deserve to be treated as our fellow-creatures.

Burns found the exercise of writing in verse to a friend congenial therapy. Revealingly, there are no fewer than seven verse-epistles in the Kilmarnock edition. His main literary model in composing these poems for Sillar, Laplaik and others was a celebrated exchange of verse-epistles between two vernacular Scottish poets of his own century, Allan Ramsay, and William Hamilton of Gilbertfield.[14] Just as his predecessors had done, Burns saw the need for those who wanted to write in Scots to encourage each other, as poets, and also as human beings. He developed a very flexible style in his verse epistles, one which allowed for the expression alike of the concerns of friendship, of personal ambition, and of social complaint. His art conceals art, so that the impression created is frequently one of wholly spontaneous, improvised composition:

> Just now I've taen the fit o' rhyme,
> My barmie noddle's working prime,
> My fancy yerket up sublime
>   Wi' hasty summon;
> Hae ye a leisure-moment's time
>   To hear what's comin?

None of Burns's contemporaries could rival such relaxed fluency. Of
the major English poets of the next century, only Byron would develop
an intimate colloquial style to compare with that of Burns the natural
communicator – as exemplified, for instance, in a passage from his first
verse-epistle to John Lapraik, in which he dismisses, in characteristic
manner, pedantry and the deadweight of learned tradition:

> I am nae *Poet*, in a sense,
> But just a *Rhymer* like by chance,
> An' hae to Learning nae pretence,
>   Yet, what the matter?
> Whene'er my Muse does on me glance,
>   I jingle at her.
>
> Your Critic-folk may cock their nose,
> And say, 'How can you e'er propose,
> You wha ken hardly *verse* frae *prose*,
>   To mak a *sang*?'
> But by your leaves, my learned foes,
>   Ye're maybe wrang.
>
> What's a' your jargon o' your Schools,
> Your Latin names for horns an' stools;
> If honest Nature made you *fools*,
>   What sairs your Grammars?
> Ye'd better taen up *spades* and *shools*,
>   Or *knappin-hammers*.
>
> A set o' dull, conceited Hashes,
> Confuse their brains in *Colledge-classes*!
> They *gang in* Stirks, and *come out* Asses,
>   Plain truth to speak;
> An' syne they think to climb Parnassus
>   By dint o' Greek!
>
> Gie me ae spark o' Nature's fire,
> That's a' the learning I desire;
> Then tho' I drudge thro' dub an' mire
>   At pleugh or cart,
> My Muse, tho' hamely in attire,
>   May touch the heart.

Just as Byron was to attain his full poetic identity only with the discovery of *ottava rima*, so Burns – from early in his career – felt especially at home with the stanza used here, 'Standart Habby'. Earlier Scottish poets had already begun to widen the range of this verse form beyond its original use for comic elegy. Burns carried the process much further, so that it became second nature with him to think of employing 'Standart Habby' in a serious poem like 'The Vision', or in a deftly controlled satire for a particular occasion like 'To a Louse', as well as in verse epistles. 'Poor Mailie's Elegy' shows that he did not lose touch with vernacular literary tradition.

It is easy to underestimate the significance of social as distinct from literary, factors inspiring Burns. With regard to song-writing, there was usually a girl, or a tune, or a joke – quite often a combination of two of these. Immediacy mattered to him. The stimulus came from a wish to please an individual, or rhyme for his own amusement, or match words to a much-loved melody. He wrote a certain number of songs in English – 'From thee, Eliza, I must go' is an example – but his instinctive wish was to use Scots words, or Scotticized English, for Scots tunes; for he had grown up in a living tradition of the playing of Scots melodies and singing of Scots songs. In his first Commonplace Book he comments directly on the suitability of Scots as the language for Scots melodies,

> There is a certain irregularity in the old Scotch Songs, a redundancy of syllables with respect to that exactness of accent & measure that the English Poetry requires, but which glides in, most melodiously with the respective tunes to which they are set. There is a degree of wild irregularity in many of the compositions & Fragments which are daily sung to them by my compeers, the common people – a certain happy arrangement of old Scotch syllables, & yet, very frequently, nothing, not even *like* rhyme, or sameness of jingle at the ends of the lines. – This has made me sometimes imagine that perhaps it might be possible for a Scotch Poet, with a nice, judicious ear, to set compositions to many of our most favourite airs, particularly that class of them mentioned above, independent of rhyme altogether.[15]

When Burns wrote about the songs being sung by the common
people daily, he had in mind casual workaday situations, as well as
occasions like the 'hearty yokin at sang about' described in his first
'Epistle to Laphaik'. One of the great attractions of song was pre-
cisely that he could hum a tune and think of words while out in the
fields. Later on, when he was a busy exciseman, hurrying about the
countryside on horseback, he would have little time to write long
poems – but songs went with him everywhere, because the tunes
were in his head. In this way, he was able to fulfil his ambition to
bring together the best of Scottish song in *The Scots Musical
Museum* (1787–1803).

Whereas in poetry Burns's main debt is to Fergusson, as a song-
writer he owes more to the example of Allan Ramsay, who wrote
songs himself and edited *The Tea-Table Miscellany*, an influential
anthology of Scots songs (1724–1737). However, despite his obli-
gation to a patriotic enthusiast who did much to make vernacular
song popular in the drawing-rooms of Edinburgh, Burns at his best
differs radically from Ramsay in his approach to the creation of song-
texts, being much more vigorous, and less inclined merely to gratify
a continuing taste for pastoral prettiness.

One song in the Kilmarnock collection which illustrates Burns's
lyrical gift is 'It was upon a Lammas night', set to the traditional
Scottish air, 'Corn Rigs'. Here his starting-point is the final song, a
mildly amusing pastoral pastiche, in Ramsay's *The Gentle Shepherd*
(1725):

> My Patie is a Lover gay,
>   His mind is never muddy;
> His breath is sweeter than new Hay,
>   His Face is fair and ruddy:
> His Shape is handsome, middle Size;
>   He's comely in his Wauking:
> The shining of his Een surprise;
>   'Tis Heaven to hear him tawking.
> Last Night I met him on a Bawk,
>   Where yellow Corn was growing,
> There mony a kindly Word he spake,
>   That set my Heart a glowing.

He kiss'd, and vow'd he wad be mine,
    And loo'd me best of ony,
That gars me like to sing since syne,
    O Corn-riggs are bonny.
Let Lasses of a silly Mind,
    Refuse what maist they're wanting;
Since we for yielding were design'd,
    We chastly should be granting.
Then I'll comply, and marry Pate,
    And syne my Cockernonny,
He's free to touzel air or late,
    Where Corn-riggs are bonny.

Guided by the tune, Burns writes out of his own experience. He turns the situation of Ramsay's song, writes from the male point of view, and conveys an unmistakable sexual swagger. He is a participant rejoicing in conquest, and his song is personal from beginning to end:

It was upon a Lammas night,
    When corn rigs are bonie,
Beneath the moon's unclouded light,
    I held awa to Annie:
The time flew by, wi' tentless head,
    Till 'tween the late and early;
Wi' sma' persuasion she agreed,
    To see me thro' the barley . . .

CHORUS

Corn rigs, an' barley rigs,
    An' corn rigs are bonie:
I'll ne'er forget that happy night,
    Amang the rigs wi' Annie.

Staying close to folk tradition, he has replaced a rather contrived, coy lyric with one which is characteristically jaunty and direct. In this way a fine melody is passed on, and Burns has simplified and deepened the communicative form.

Burns's world-wide popularity owes much to the simplicity of utterance of songs like 'It was upon a Lammas night'. It is sometimes forgotten, however, that his distinctive 'voice', whether in lyric or satire, resulted from commitment to his art, as well as from an immediately attractive personal candour. He is in no sense a provincial simpleton or mere literary curiosity. His is an achieved simplicity: because he had true things to say and wanted to share his ideas, he had worked his way through the traps of poetic artifice which caught so many British poets in his century. Credit for the renewal of energy and simplicity in British poetry in the late eighteenth century tends to be given automatically to Blake, Coleridge and Wordsworth alone, by English and American critics who assume that the use of Scots disqualifies Burns from full consideration. But the dates of original publication speak for themselves. Two hundred years on, the range and quality of Burns's poetic achievement in the 1786 volume seem more impressive than ever.

1. Burns to Dr J. Moore, 2 August 1787, *Letters of Robert Burns*, ed. J. De Lancey Ferguson and G. Ross Roy (1985), I. 143. (Moore, 1729–1802, was a widely travelled Scots doctor and man of letters, with his medical practice in London. His first novel *Zeluco* (1786) had considerable success, and was to provide Byron with hints for the character of Childe Harold. He was father of Sir John Moore, hero of Corunna.)
2. Burns to Moore, *Letters*, op. cit., I. 144–5.
3. *The Works of Robert Burns*, ed. James Currie, 2nd edition (1801), vol. iii, pp. 380–1.
4. John Butt, *The Mid-Eighteenth Century* (*Oxford History of English Literature*, vol. viii, 1979), p. 159.
5. Burns to Moore, *Letters*, op. cit., I. 143.
6. On Wilson, see Frances M. Thomson, 'John Wilson, an Ayrshire printer, publisher and bookseller', *The Bibliotheck*, vol. v (1967–70), pp. 41–61; and Farquhar McKenzie, 'John Wilson, 1759–1821', *Burns Chronicle*, 3rd series, vol. xxii (1973), pp. 1–5.
7. 'April 14th, 1786. / PROPOSALS, / FOR PUBLISHING BY SUBSCRIPTION, / SCOTCH POEMS, / BY ROBERT BURNS. / The Work to be elegantly printed in One Volume, Octavo. Price Stitched *Three Shillings*. As the Author has not the most distant *Mercenary* view in

Publishing, as soon as so many Subscribers appear as will defray the *necessary* Expence, / The Work will be sent to the Press. / Set out the brunt side o' your shin, / For pride in *Poets* is nae sin; / *Glory's* the Prize for which *they* rin, / And *Fame's* their jo; / And wha blaws best the Horn shall win: / And wharefore no? Ramsay.' The only known surviving copy of Burns's *Proposals* is in the Burns Cottage Museum, Alloway.

8. 'A Memoir of the Life of the Late Robert Burns' (1797); D. A. Low, ed., *Robert Burns: The Critical Heritage* (1974), p. 122. On the evidence for and against 31 July as the date of publication, see J. W. Egerer, *A Bibliography of Robert Burns* (1964), p. 4.

9. Burns to Moore, *Letters*, op. cit., I. 145; and cf. letter to Robert Aiken, c. 8 October 1786 (*Letters*, op. cit., I. 57): 'I was with Wilson, my printer, t'other day, and settled all our bygone matters between us. After I paid him all demands, I made him the offer of the second edition, on the hazard of being paid out of *the first and readiest*, which he declines. By his account, the paper of a thousand copies would cost about twenty-seven pounds, and the printing about fifteen or sixteen: he offers to agree to this for the printing, if I will advance for the paper, but this you know is out of my power; so farewell hopes of a second edition till I grow richer! an epocha which, I think, will arrive at the payment of the British national debt.' Wilson's account for printing the Kilmarnock edition is reproduced in J. D. Ross, *The Story of the Kilmarnock Burns* (1933), pp. 59–60.

10. F. B. Snyder, *The Life of Robert Burns* (1932), p. 154.

11. Burns to Moore, *Letters*, op. cit., I. 145.

12. Mackenzie's *Lounger* essay is reprinted, along with the comments of other contemporaries of Burns cited in this paragraph, in D. A. Low, ed., *Robert Burns: The Critical Heritage* (1974).

13. For a detailed account of Burns's handling of Scots, see David Murison's essay 'The Language of Burns' in D. A. Low, ed., *Critical Essays on Robert Burns* (1975), pp. 54–69. Murison notes that 'in his complete works he employs over 2,000 peculiarly Scots words (the average Scots speaker today would have about 500 at the most)' (p. 63).

14. The 'familiar epistles' exchanged by Hamilton and Ramsay are reprinted in the Scottish Text Society edition of *The Works of Allan Ramsay*, vol. i (ed. Burns Martin and John W. Oliver, 1951), pp. 115–37.

15. *Robert Burns's Commonplace Book, 1783–5*, ed. J. C. Ewing and D. Cook (Glasgow, 1938), reprinted with introduction by David Daiches (1965), p. 38.

Select Bibliography

Texts

Poems, Chiefly in the Scottish Dialect (Kilmarnock, 1786). No previous modern edition, but frequently reissued in facsimile. See G. Ross Roy, 'Some notes on the facsimiles of the Kilmarnock Burns', The Bibliotheck, vol. iv (1963–6). Recent facsimiles include those by the Scolar Press (Menston, 1971; also prints the poems which Burns added in 1787), and by Famedram (Gartocharn, [1977]).

The Poems and Songs of Robert Burns, ed. James Kinsley, 3 vols. (Oxford, 1968). The standard complete edition of Burns's poetry, chronologically arranged.

The Letters of Robert Burns, ed. J. De Lancey Ferguson and G. Ross Roy, 2 vols. (Oxford, 1985). The standard edition of the poet's correspondence, now completely revised.

Robert Burns's Commonplace Book, 1783–85, ed. J. C. Ewing and D. Cook (Glasgow, 1938); repr., with introduction by D. Daiches (London, 1965). Offers fascinating insights into the making of the poet.

Biography and Criticism

Mary Ellen Brown, Burns and Tradition (London, 1984). A study of Burns's relationship to folk tradition, including his role as collector and editor of Scottish song.

Thomas Crawford, Burns: A Study of the Poems and Songs (Edinburgh, 1960, repr. 1978). Contains the most detailed critical analysis to date.

Thomas Crawford, Society and the Lyric. A Study of the Song Culture of Eighteenth-Century Scotland (Edinburgh, 1979). Shows how Burns's songs were the culmination of a rich song tradition.

David Daiches, Robert Burns (1950, rev. 1966, repr. 1981). Lively biographical and critical study.

Catarina Ericson-Roos, The Songs of Robert Burns: A Study of the Unity of Poetry and Music (Uppsala, 1977). Valuable for its emphasis on song as an integrated art form.

J. W. Egerer, A Bibliography of Robert Burns (Edinburgh, 1964). Aims to list every significant original appearance of poetry or prose to 1802; most 'complete' editions to 1953.

R. D. S. Jack and Andrew Noble (ed.) The Art of Robert Burns (London and Totowa, N.J., 1982). A wide-ranging collection of critical essays.

James Kinsley, *Burns and the Peasantry, 1785*, Warton Lecture on English Poetry, British Academy, 1974. Stimulating on Burns as 'social poet'.

Maurice Lindsay, *The Burns Encyclopaedia*, 3rd edition (London, 1980). A useful reference work, by the author of *Robert Burns: The Man, His Work, The Legend* (1954, rev. 1979).

Donald A. Low (ed.), *Robert Burns: The Critical Heritage* (London and Boston, 1974). Includes the first reviews and much early criticism.

Donald A. Low (ed.), *Critical Essays on Robert Burns* (London and Boston, 1974). Considers various aspects of Burns's achievement as poet and song-writer.

David Murison, *The Guid Scots Tongue* (Edinburgh, 1977). A helpful introductory guide to Lowland Scots, by a former editor of *The Scottish National Dictionary*, 10 vols., 1929–76.

Franklyn B. Snyder, *The Life of Robert Burns* (New York, 1932; repr. Hamden, Conn., 1968). Still the most thoroughly documented life of the poet.

John Strawhorn (ed.), *Ayrshire in the Time of Robert Burns* (Ayr, 1959). Valuable sourcebook on Burns's regional background.

Map

Armstrongs' Map of Ayrshire (1775), in six sheets. Facsimile published by Ayrshire Archaeological & Natural History Society.

Cassette

Poems chiefly in the Scottish dialect: a selection from the Kilmarnock Edition read by members of the Irvine Burns Club, Scotsoun (1975) SSC IBC 008.

Note on the Text

The text used throughout as copy for this edition is that published in *Poems, Chiefly In the Scottish Dialect* (1786). While not a facsimile, the Everyman edition seeks to be faithful in its essentials to the original. Burns's carefully revised holograph manuscripts of six poems ('The Twa Dogs', 'Scotch Drink', 'The Author's Earnest Cry and Prayer', 'The Holy Fair', 'Address to the Deil' and 'The Cotter's Saturday Night'), used as printer's copy in 1786 and now in the safe keeping of Irvine Burns Club, have been consulted. Capitals, italics and other features which clearly belong in an integral way to the Kilmarnock edition text have been retained. Single rather than double inverted commas have been used to enclose reported speech and quotations, 'its' and 'it's' have been conventionally differentiated, and minor printing errors have been silently corrected (cf. list by D. McNaught in the *Burns Chronicle*, vol. xix, 1910, pp. 75–6).

Titles of individual poems are given in full in the text. Some have been shortened on the Contents pages, e.g. 'The Twa Dogs' for 'The Twa Dogs, A Tale'. All footnotes in the text are Burns's own as printed in 1786. The letter (B) in the margin of a poem denotes the poet's explanation of the meaning of a Scots word or phrase in his 1786 (or expanded 1787) Glossary.

Appendix C contains a finding-list of poetic manuscripts. Some of the more significant textual changes made by the poet before or after first publication are cited in the notes; but no attempt has been made to duplicate James Kinsley's exhaustive study of early textual variants (1968). It is worth noting that one important group of manuscripts is published in its entirety in *Burns Holograph Manuscripts in the Kilmarnock Monument Museum*, ed. David Sneddon, Kilmarnock, 1889.

Burns's Scots

The marginal glosses which accompany the text of the Scots poems in this edition aim to gloss, on its first occurrence in each poem, every word which is likely to be unfamiliar to the modern reader. To avoid unnecessary repetition, the most common words are given in the list below. Most of the words listed are variant forms of words which are well known in English, but a few Lowland Scots words without equivalent English forms (e.g. 'unco') are included. Burns's own glossary, as printed in 1786, is reproduced in Appendix A, and the poet's use of Lowland Scots is fully discussed in the introduction.

List of Common Words

a' *all*
ae *one*
aff *off*
aft(en) *often*
amaist *almost*
amang *among*
ance *once*
ane *one*
auld *old*
awa *away*
ay(e) *always*
baith *both*
ben *indoors/within*
bluid *blood*
bon(n)ie *attractive*
braw *fine/splendid*
ca' *call/name*
cauld *cold*
countra *country*
fa' *fall*
frae *from*
gae, gaen, gaun *go, gone*
gang *etc go*
gat *got*
gie *etc give*
guid *good*
hae *have*
hame *home*
ither, *other, each other*
ilk(a) *each/every*
ken *know*

lang(er) *long(er)*
mair *more*
maist *most, almost*
maun *must*
meikle/mickle/muckle *much*
monie/mony *many*
na, nae, nane, naething *not, no, none, nothing*
onie/ony *any*
owre *over, too*
sae *so*
sang *song*
sic/sich *such*
sma' *small*
tae *to*
taen *taken*
thegither *together*
tither *the other*
twa *two*
unco *very, odd*
wa' *wall*
wad *would, would have*
wee *small*
weel *well*
wha/whase *who, whose*
whare *where*
why(i)les *now, at times/ sometimes*
yon *that*

POEMS,

CHIEFLY IN THE SCOTTISH DIALECT
(KILMARNOCK, 1786)

THE TWA DOGS, A TALE

'TWAS in that place o' Scotland's isle,
That bears the name o' auld king COIL,
Upon a bonie day in June,
When wearing thro' the afternoon,
Twa Dogs, that were na thrang at hame,   busy
Forgather'd ance upon a time.

 The first I'll name, they ca'd him *Caesar*,
Was keepet for His Honor's pleasure;
His hair, his size, his mouth, his lugs,   ears
10 Shew'd he was nane o' Scotland's dogs,
But whalpet some place far abroad,   whelped
Where sailors gang to fish for Cod.

 His locked, letter'd, braw brass-collar
Shew'd him the *gentleman* an' *scholar*;
But tho' he was o' high degree,
The fient a pride na pride had he,   not a bit of
But wad hae spent an hour caressan,
Ev'n wi' a Tinkler-gipsey's *messan*:   mongrel
At Kirk or Market, Mill or Smiddie,   church, smithy
20 Nae tawted *tyke*, tho' e'er sae duddie,   matted cur, ragged
But he wad stan't, as glad to see him,   stood
An' stroan't on stanes an' hillocks wi' him. watered, stones

 The tither was a *ploughman's collie*,
A rhyming, ranting, raving billie,   merry, fellow
Wha for his friend an' comrade had him,
And in his freaks had *Luath* ca'd him,   odd notions
After some dog in *Highland sang,
Was made lang syne, lord knows how lang. long ago

*Cuchullin's dog in Ossian's Fingal.

He was a gash an' faithfu' *tyke*,   wise, dog
30 As ever lap a sheugh or dyke.   leapt, ditch, stone wall
His honest, sonsie, baws'nt face   pleasant, white-striped
Ay gat him friends in ilka place;
His breast was white, his towzie back,   shaggy
Weel clad wi' coat o' glossy black;
His gawsie tail, wi' upward curl,   cheerful
Hung owre his hurdies wi' a swirl.   buttocks

Nae doubt but they were fain o' ither,   fond of
An' unco pack an' thick thegither;   very intimate together
Wi' social nose whyles snuff'd an' snowket;   sniffed, poked about
40 Whyles mice and modewurks they howket;   moles, dug
Whyles scour'd awa in lang excursion,   ranged
An' worry'd ither in diversion;
Till tir'd at last wi' mony a farce,
They set them down upon their arse,
An' there began a lang digression
About the *lords o' the creation*.

CAESAR

I've aften wonder'd, honest *Luath*,
What sort o' life poor dogs like you have;
An' when the *gentry's* life I saw,
50 What way *poor bodies* liv'd ava.   folk, at all

Our *Laird* gets in his racked rents,
His coals, his kane, an' a' his stents: payment in kind, dues
He rises when he likes himsel;
His flunkies answer at the bell;
He ca's his coach; he ca's his horse;
He draws a bonie, silken purse
As lang's my tail, whare thro' the steeks,   stitches
The yellow letter'd *Geordie* keeks.   guinea, peeps

Frae morn to een it's nought but toiling,   evening
60 At baking, roasting, frying, boiling;
An' tho' the gentry first are steghan,   cramming

Yet ev'n the *ha' folk* fill their peghan   servants, stomach
Wi' sauce, ragouts, an' sic like trashtrie,   trash
That's little short o' downright wastrie.   waste/extravagance
Our *Whipper-in*, wee, blastet wonner,   hunt-servant,
                                                                                   wonder
Poor worthless elf, it eats a dinner,
Better than ony *Tenant-man*
His Honor has in a' the lan':
An' what poor *Cot-folk* pit their painch in,   cottagers, put,
                                                                                            paunch
70   I own it's past my comprehension.

LUATH
   Trowth, Caesar, whyles they're fash't enough;   indeed, troubled
A *Cotter* howkan in a sheugh,
Wi' dirty stanes biggan a dyke,   building
Bairan a quarry, an' sic like,   clearing
Himsel, a wife, he thus sustains,
A smytrie o' wee, duddie weans,   swarm, children
An' nought but his han'-daurk, to keep   labour of his hands
Them right an' tight in thack an' raep.   thatch and rope

   An' when they meet wi' sair disasters,   sore
80   Like loss o' health or want o' masters,
Ye maist wad think, a wee touch langer,
An' they maun starve o' cauld and hunger:
But how it comes, I never kent yet,
They're maistly wonderfu' contented;
An' buirdly chiels, and clever hizzies,   well-built lads,
                                                                              wenches
Are bred in sic a way as this is.

CAESAR
   But then, to see how ye're negleket,
How huff'd, an' cuff'd, an' disrespeket!   scolded
L—d man, our gentry care as little
90   For *delvers*, *ditchers*, an' sic cattle;   beasts
They gang as saucy by poor folk,
As I wad by a stinkan brock.   badger

I've notic'd, on our Laird's *court-day*,   rent-day
An' mony a time my heart's been wae,   sad
Poor *tenant bodies*, scant o' cash,
How they maun thole a *factor's* snash;   endure, insolence
He'll stamp an' threaten, curse an' swear,
He'll *apprehend* them, *poind* their gear;   seize, distrain
While they maun stan', wi' aspect humble,
100 An' hear it a', an' fear an' tremble!

I see how folk live that hae riches;
But surely poor-folk maun be wretches!

LUATH

They're no sae wretched's ane wad think;   as one would
Tho' constantly on poortith's brink,   poverty
They're sae accustom'd wi' the sight,
The view o't gies them little fright.

Then chance and fortune are sae guided,
They're ay in less or mair provided;
And tho' fatigu'd wi' close employment,
110 A blink o' rest's a sweet enjoyment.

The dearest comfort o' their lives,
Their grushie weans an' faithfu' wives;   thriving
The *prattling things* are just their pride,
That sweetens a' their fire side.

An' whyles twalpennie-worth o' *nappy*   twelvepenny, ale
Can mak the bodies unco happy;   folk
They lay aside their private cares,
To mind the Kirk and State affairs;
They'll talk o' *patronage* an' *priests*,
120 Wi' kindling fury i' their breasts,
Or tell what new taxation's comin,
An' ferlie at the folk in LON'ON.   marvel

As bleak-fac'd Hallowmass returns,
They get the jovial, rantan *Kirns*,   harvest-homes
When *rural life*, of ev'ry station,
Unite in common recreation;
Love blinks, Wit slaps, an' social Mirth
Forgets there's *care* upo' the earth.

That *merry day* the year begins,
130 They bar the door on frosty win's;
The nappy reeks wi' mantling ream,   smokes, foam
An' sheds a heart-inspiring steam;
The luntan pipe, an' sneeshin mill,   smoking, snuff-box
Are handed round wi' right guid will;
The cantie, auld folks, crackan crouse,   lively, talking
The young anes rantan thro' the house——   cheerfully
My heart has been sae fain to see them,   romping
That I for joy hae barket wi' them.   glad

Still it's owre true that ye hae said,
140 Sic game is now owre aften play'd;   often
There's monie a creditable *stock*
O' decent, honest, fawsont folk,   respectable
Are riven out baith root an' branch,   torn
Some rascal's pridefu' greed to quench,
Wha thinks to knit himsel the faster
In favor wi' some *gentle Master*,
Wha aiblins thrang a *parliamentin*,   perhaps
For Britain's guid his saul indentin——   soul, pledging

CAESAR
Haith lad ye little ken about it;   'a petty oath' (B)
150 *For Britain's guid*! guid faith! I doubt it.
Say rather, gaun as PREMIERS lead him,   going
An' saying *aye* or *no's* they bid him:
At Operas an' Plays parading,
Mortgaging, gambling, masquerading:

Or maybe, in a frolic daft,
To HAGUE or CALAIS takes a waft,   sea-trip
To make a *tour* an' tak a whirl,   go on the Grand Tour
To learn *bon ton* an' see the worl'.

160   There, at VIENNA or VERSAILLES,
He rives his father's auld entails;   splits, estate succession
Or by MADRID he takes the rout,   road
To thrum *guittars* an' fecht wi' nowt;   fight, cattle
Or down *Italian Vista* startles,
Wh-re-hunting amang groves o' myrtles:
Then bowses drumlie *German-water*,   boozes, cloudy
To mak himsel look fair and fatter,
An' purge the bitter ga's an' cankers,   galls
O' curst *Venetian* b-res an' ch-ncres.   cracks, ulcers

For Britain's guid! for her destruction!
170   Wi' dissipation, feud an' faction!

LUATH

Hech man! dear sirs! is that the gate,   way
They waste sae mony a braw estate!
Are we sae foughten and harass'd   worn out
For gear to gang that gate at last!   wealth

O would they stay aback frae courts,
An' please themsels wi' countra sports,
It wad for ev'ry ane be better,
The *Laird*, the *Tenant*, an' the *Cotter*!
For thae frank, rantan, ramblan billies,   these
180   Fient haet o' them's ill hearted fellows;   not one
Except for breakin o' their timmer,   timber
Or speakin lightly o' their *Limmer*,   mistress
Or shootin of a hare or moorcock,
The ne'er-a-bit they're ill to poor folk.   not in the least

But will ye tell me, master *Caesar*,
Sure *great folk's* life's a life o' pleasure?
Nae cauld nor hunger e'er can steer them,   affect
The vera thought o't need na fear them.   frighten

CAESAR

L—d man, were ye but whyles where I am,
190   The *gentles* ye wad neer envy them!   'great folks' (B)

It's true, they need na starve or sweat,
Thro' Winter's cauld, or Summer's heat;
They've nae sair-wark to craze their banes,   hard work, bones
An' fill *auld-age* wi' grips an' granes;   gripes and groans
But *human-bodies* are sic fools,
For a' their colledges an' schools,
That when nae *real* ills perplex them,
They *mak* enow themsels to vex them;   enough
An' ay the less they hae to sturt them,   trouble
200   In like proportion, less will hurt them.

A country fellow at the pleugh,   plough
His *acre's* till'd, he's right eneugh;
A country girl at her wheel,
Her *dizzen's* done, she's unco weel;   dozen cuts of yarn
But Gentlemen, an' Ladies warst,   worst of all
Wi' ev'n down *want o'wark* are curst.   sheer lack of
                                                            work
They loiter, lounging, lank an' lazy;
Tho' deil-haet ails them, yet uneasy;   damn-all
Their days, insipid, dull an' tasteless,
210   Their nights, unquiet, lang an' restless.

An' ev'n their sports, their balls an' races
Their galloping thro' public places,
There's sic parade, sic pomp an' art,
The joy can scarcely reach the heart.

The *Men* cast out in *party-matches*, — fall out, card-contests
Then sowther a' in deep debauches. — patch up
Ae night, they're mad wi' drink an' wh-ring,
Niest day their life is past enduring. — next

The *Ladies* arm-in-arm in clusters,
220 As great an' gracious a' as sisters;
But hear their *absent thoughts* o' ither,
They're a' run deils an' jads thegither. — all complete hussies
Whyles, owre the wee bit cup an' platie,
They sip the *scandal-potion* pretty;
Or lee-lang nights, wi' crabbet leuks, — live-long, cross looks
Pore owre the devil's *pictur'd beuks*; — playing-cards
Stake on a chance a farmer's stackyard,
An' cheat like ony *unhang'd blackguard*.

There's some exceptions, man an' woman;
230 But this is Gentry's life in common.

By this, the sun was out o' sight,
An' darker gloamin brought the night: — twilight
The *bum-clock* humm'd wi' lazy drone, — beetle
The kye stood rowtan i' the loan; — cattle, lowing, pasture
When up they gat an' shook their lugs,
Rejoic'd they were na *men* but *dogs*;
And each took off his several way,
Resolv'd to meet some ither day.

SCOTCH DRINK

Gie him strong Drink *until he wink,*
That's sinking in despair;
An' liquor *guid to fire his bluid,*
That's prest wi' grief an' care:
There let him bowse an' deep carouse,
Wi' bumpers flowing o'er,
Till he forgets his loves *or debts,*
An' minds his griefs no more.

Solomon's Proverbs, xxxi. 6, 7

LET other Poets raise a fracas
'Bout vines, an' wines, an' druken *Bacchus*,   drunken
An' crabbed names an' stories wrack us,   ill-natured
  An' grate our lug,   ear
I sing the juice *Scotch bear* can mak us,   barley
  In glass or jug.

O thou, my MUSE! guid, auld SCOTCH DRINK!
Whether thro' wimplin worms thou jink,   twisting tubes, slip fast
Or, richly brown, ream owre the brink,   froth
10 In glorious faem,   foam
Inspire me, till I *lisp* an' *wink*,
  To sing thy name!

Let husky Wheat the haughs adorn,   level land by a river
And Aits set up their awnie horn,   oats, bearded
An' Pease an' Beans, at een or morn,   evening
  Perfume the plain,
Leeze me on thee *John Barleycorn*,   you delight me
  Thou king o' grain!

On thee aft Scotland chows her cood,   chews, cud
20 In souple scones, the wale o' food!   pliable, choice
Or tumbling in the boiling flood
  Wi' kail an' beef;   vegetable broth
But when thou pours thy strong *heart's blood*,
  There thou shines chief.

Food fills the wame, an' keeps us livin;   stomach
Tho' life's a gift no worth receivin,
When heavy-dragg'd wi' pine an' grievin;
      But oil'd by thee,
The wheels o' life gae down-hill, scrievin,   gliding swiftly
30   Wi' rattlin glee.

Thou clears the head o' doited Lear;   stupified learning
Thou chears the heart o' drooping Care;
Thou strings the nerves o' Labor-sair,   -hard
      At's weary toil;
Thou ev'n brightens dark Despair,
      Wi' gloomy smile.

Aft, clad in massy, siller weed,   silver dress
Wi' Gentles thou erects thy head;   'great folks' (B)
Yet humbly kind, in time o' need,
40   The *poor man's* wine;
His wee drap pirratch, or his bread,   drop of, porridge
      Thou kitchens fine.   seasons

Thou art the life o' public haunts;
But thee, what were our fairs and rants?   without, sprees
Ev'n godly meetings o' the saunts,   saints/'the elect'
      By thee inspir'd,
When gaping they besiege the *tents*,   'field pulpit' (B)
      Are doubly fir'd.

That *merry night* we get the corn in,
50 O sweetly, then, thou reams the horn in!   horn vessel
Or reekan on a *New-year-mornin*   smoking
      In cog or bicker,   wooden drinking cups
An' just a wee drap *sp'ritual burn* in,   water used in brewing
      An gusty sucker!   tasty sugar

When Vulcan gies his bellys breath,
An' Ploughmen gather wi' their graith,   ploughing gear
O rare! to see thee fizz an' freath   froth
   I' the lugget caup!   wooden dish with handles
Then *Burnewin* comes on like Death   'burn-wind'/ blacksmith
60   At ev'ry chap.   stroke

Nae mercy, then, for airn or steel;   iron
The brawnie, banie, ploughman-chiel   bony, -lad
Brings hard owrehip, wi' sturdy wheel,   over the hip
   The strong forehammer,   sledge-hammer
Till block an' studdie ring an' reel   anvil
   Wi' dinsome clamour.   noisy

When skirlin weanies see the light,   yelling infants
Thou maks the gossips clatter bright,   neighbour-women chatter
How fumbling coofs their dearies slight,   clowns
70   Wae worth them for't!   cursed be
While healths gae round to him wha, *tight*,   virile
   Gies famous sport.   gives

When neebors anger at a plea,   neighbours
An' just as wud as wud can be,   angry
How easy can the *barley-brie*   whisky
   Cement the quarrel!
It's aye the cheapest Lawyer's fee
   To taste the barrel.

Alake! that e'er my *Muse* has reason,
80   To wyte her countrymen wi' treason!   blame
But monie daily weet their weason   wet, gullet
   Wi' liquors nice,
An' hardly, in a winter season,
   E'er spier her price.   ask

Wae worth that *Brandy*, burnan trash!
Fell source o' monie a pain an' brash!   severe, illness
Twins monie a poor, doylt, druken hash   deprives, muddled, drunken waster
    O' half his days;
An' sends, beside, auld *Scotland's* cash
90   To her warst faes.   worst foes

Ye Scots wha wish auld Scotland well,
Ye chief, to you my tale I tell,
Poor, plackless devils like *mysel*,   penniless
    It sets you ill,
Wi' bitter, dearthfu' *wines* to mell,   meddle
    Or foreign gill.   measure

May *Gravels* round his blather wrench,   urinary pains, bladder
An' *Gouts* torment him, inch by inch,
Wha twists his gruntle wi' a glunch   snout, frown
100   O' sour disdain,
Out owre a glass o' *Whisky-punch*
    Wi' honest men!

O *Whisky*! soul o' plays an' pranks!
Accept a *Bardie's* gratefu' thanks!   poet's
When wanting thee, what tuneless cranks   noises
    Are my poor Verses!
Thou comes—— they rattle i' their ranks
    At ither's arses!

Thee *Ferintosh*! O sadly lost!   a whisky
110 Scotland lament frae coast to coast!
Now colic-grips, an' barkin hoast,   cough
    May kill us a';
For loyal Forbes' *Charter'd boast*
    Is ta'en awa!

Thae curst horse-leeches o' th'Excise,   those
Wha mak the *Whisky stells* their prize!   stills
Haud up thy han' *Diel*! ance, twice, *thrice*!   hold, Devil
    There, sieze the blinkers!   spies/cheats
An' bake them up in brunstane pies   brimstone
120   For poor d—n'd *Drinkers*.

Fortune, if thou'll but gie me still   give
Hale breeks, a scone, an' *whisky gill*,   intact breeches
An' rowth o' *rhyme* to rave at will,   abundance
    Tak a' the rest,
An' deal't about as thy blind skill
    Directs thee best.

THE AUTHOR'S EARNEST CRY AND PRAYER, TO THE RIGHT HONORABLE AND HONORABLE, THE SCOTCH REPRESENTATIVES IN THE HOUSE OF COMMONS

Dearest of Distillation! last and best! ——
—— *How art thou lost!* ——

          Parody on Milton

YE *Irish lords*, ye *knights* an' *squires*,
Wha *represent* our *Brughs* an' *Shires*,   burghs
An' dousely manage our affairs   decorously
    In *Parliament*,
To you a simple Bardie's pray'rs   poet's
    Are humbly sent.

Alas! my roupet *Muse* is haerse!   husky, hoarse
Your Honors' hearts wi' grief 'twad pierce,   it would
To see her sittan on her arse
10   Low i' the dust,
An' scriechan out prosaic verse,   screeching
    An' like to brust!   burst

Tell them wha hae the chief direction,
Scotland an' *me's* in great affliction,
E'er sin' they laid that curst restriction
  On AQUAVITAE;   *water of life/ whisky*
An' rouse them up to strong conviction,
  An' move their pity.

Stand forth and tell yon PREMIER YOUTH,
20 The honest, open, naked truth:
Tell him o' mine an' Scotland's drouth,   *thirst*
  His servants humble:
The muckle devil blaw you south,   *great, blow*
  If ye dissemble!

Does ony *great man* glunch an' gloom?   *frown*
Speak out an' never fash your thumb.   *pay heed/bother*
Let *posts* an' *pensions* sink or swoom   *swim*
  Wi' them wha grant them:
If honestly they canna come,
30   Far better want them.

In gath'rin votes you were na slack,
Now stand as tightly by your tack: *leasehold/tenure*
Ne'er claw your lug, an' fidge your back,   *scratch, ear, shrug*
  An' hum an' haw,
But raise your arm, an' tell your crack   *story/scandalous tale*
  Before them a'.

Paint Scotland greetan owre her thrissle;   *weeping, thistle*
Her *mutchkin stowp* as toom's a whissle;   *¼-pint measure, empty as, whistle*
An' d—mn'd Excise-men in a bussle   *commotion*
40   Seizan a *Stell*,   *still*
Triumphant crushan't like a muscle   *crushing it, mussel*
   Or laimpet shell.   *limpet*

Then on the tither hand present her,
A blackguard *Smuggler*, right behint her,
An' cheek-for-chow, a chuffie Vintner,   -by-jowl, fat-faced
      Colleaguing join,   conspiring
Picking her pouch as bare as Winter,
      Of a' kind coin.

Is there, that bears the name o' SCOT,
50 But feels his heart's bluid rising hot,   blood
To see his poor, auld Mither's *pot*,
      Thus dung in staves,   beaten into
An' plunder'd o' her hindmost groat,
      By gallows knaves?

Alas! I'm but a nameless wight,   fellow
Trode i' the mire out o' sight!
But could I like MONTGOMERIES fight,
      Or gab like BOSWELL,   talk eloquently
There's some *sark-necks* I wad *draw* tight, collars
60   An' *tye* some *hose* well.

God bless your Honors, can ye see't,
The kind, auld, cantie Carlin greet,   pleasant old
                      woman, weep
An' no get warmly to your feet,
      An' gar them hear it,   get them to
An' tell them, wi' a patriot-heat,
      Ye winna bear it?   will not

Some o' you nicely ken the laws,
To round the period an' pause,
An' with rhetoric clause on clause
70   To mak harangues;
Then echo thro' Saint Stephen's wa's
      Auld Scotland's wrangs.   wrongs

Dempster, a true-blue Scot I'se warran;   I will warrant
Thee, aith-detesting, chaste *Kilkerran*;   oath-
An' that glib-gabbet Highland Baron,   smooth-tongued
     The Laird o' *Graham*;
And ane, a chap that's d—mn'd auldfarran,   old-fashioned/ 'sagacious'
     Dundas his name.

Erskine, a spunkie norland billie;   spirited northern lad
80 True Campbells, *Frederick* an' *Ilay*;
An' Livistone, the bauld *Sir Willie*;   bold
     An' monie ithers,
Whom auld Demosthenes or Tully   Cicero
     Might own for brithers.   brothers

Arouse my boys! exert your mettle,
To get auld Scotland back her *kettle*!   cauldron
Or faith! I'll wad my new pleugh-pettle,   wager, plough-spade
     Ye'll see't or lang,   before long
She'll teach you, wi' a reekan whittle,   smoking knife
90   Anither sang.

This while she's been in crankous mood,   captious
Her *lost Militia* fir'd her bluid;
(Deil na they never mair do guid,   May they never prosper at all
     Play'd her that pliskie!)   [who], trick
An' now she's like to rin red-wud   run stark mad
     About her *Whisky*.

An' L—d! if ance they pit her till't,   put, to it
Her tartan petticoat she'll kilt,
An' durk an' pistol at her belt,   dirk
100   She'll tak the streets,   take to
An' rin her whittle to the hilt,   run
     I' th' first she meets!

For G—d-sake, Sirs! then speak her fair,
An' straik her cannie wi' the hair,   stroke gently
An' to the *muckle house* repair,   Parliament
      Wi' instant speed,
An' strive, wi' a your Wit an' Lear,   Learning
      To get remead.   redress

110   Yon ill-tongu'd tinkler, *Charlie Fox*,   that low tinker/ rascal
May taunt you wi' his jeers an' mocks;
But gie him't het, my hearty cocks!   hot
      E'en cowe the cadie!   trounce, rascal
An' send him to his dicing box,
      An' sportin lady.

Tell yon guid bluid o' auld *Boconnock's*,
I'll be his debt twa mashlum bonnocks,   mixed meal bannocks
An' drink his health in auld **Nanse Tinnock's*
      Nine times a week,
If he some scheme, like tea an' winnocks,   windows
120   Wad kindly seek.

Could he some *commutation* broach,
I'll pledge my aith in guid braid Scotch,   broad Scots
He need na fear their foul reproach
      Nor erudition,
Yon mixtie-maxtie, queer hotch-potch,   confused
      The *Coalition*.

Auld Scotland has a raucle tongue;   rough
She's just a devil wi' a rung;   cudgel
An' if she promise auld or young
130   To tak their part,
Tho' by the neck she should be strung,
      She'll no desert.

---

*A worthy old Hostess of the Author's in *Mauchline*, where he sometimes studies Politics over a glass of guid, auld *Scotch Drink*.

And now, ye chosen FIVE AND FORTY,
May still your Mither's heart support ye;   mother's
Then, tho' a *Minister* grow dorty,   supercilious
       An' kick your place,
Ye'll snap your fingers, poor an' hearty,
       Before his face.

God bless your Honors, a' your days,   sups, broth, rags,
140 Wi' sowps o' kail and brats o' claise,   clothes
In spite o' a' the thievish kaes   jackdaws
       That haunt St *Jamie's*!
Your humble Bardie sings an' prays
       While *Rab* his name is.

POSTSCRIPT

Let half-starv'd slaves in warmer skies,
See future wines, rich-clust'ring, rise;
Their lot auld Scotland ne'er envies,
       But blythe an' frisky,
She eyes her freeborn, martial boys,
150   Tak aff their Whisky.   drink

What tho' their Phoebus kinder warms,
While Fragrance blooms an' Beauty charms!
When wretches range, in famish'd swarms,
       The scented groves,
Or hounded forth, *dishonor* arms
       In hungry droves.

Their *gun's* a burden on their shouther;   shoulder
They downa bide the stink o' *powther*;   cannot endure,
Their bauldest thought's a hank'ring swither,   powder
160   To stan' or rin,   boldest, hesitant
Till skelp— a shot— they're aff, a' throw'ther,   uncertainty
       To save their skin.   smack, in
       confusion

But bring a SCOTCHMAN frae his hill,
Clap in his cheek a *Highland gill*,   quarter mutchkin
Say, such is royal GEORGE'S will,

An' there's the foe,
He has nae thought but how to kill
    Twa at a blow.

Nae cauld, faint-hearted doubtings tease him;
170 Death comes, wi' fearless eye he sees him;
Wi' bluidy han' a welcome gies him;
    An' when he fa's,   falls
His latest draught o' breathin lea'es him   leaves
    In faint huzzas.

Sages their solemn een may steek,   eyes, shut
An' raise a philosophic reek,   smoke
An' physically causes seek,
    In *clime* an' *season*,
But tell me *Whisky's* name in Greek,
180   I'll tell the reason.

SCOTLAND, my auld, respected Mither!
Tho' whyles ye moistify your leather,   moisten, throat
Till whare ye sit, on craps o' heather   tops
    Ye tine your dam;   lose [i.e. pass water]
FREEDOM and WHISKY gang thegither,
    Tak aff your *dram*!

THE HOLY FAIR

A robe of seeming truth and trust
  Hid crafty observation;
And secret hung, with poison'd crust,
  The dirk of Defamation:
A mask that like the gorget show'd,
  Dye-varying, on the pigeon;
And for a mantle large and broad,
  He wrapt him in Religion.

                    Hypocrisy A-La-Mode

I

UPON a simmer Sunday morn,   summer
  When Nature's face is fair,
I walked forth to view the corn,
  An' snuff the callor air.   sniff, fresh
The rising sun, owre GALSTON Muirs,   over
  Wi' glorious light was glintan;
The hares were hirplan down the furrs,   moving unevenly forward, furrows
  The lav'rocks they were chantan   larks
        Fu' sweet that day.   very

II

10 As lightsomely I glowr'd abroad   gazed intently
  To see a scene sae gay,
Three *hizzies*, early at the road,   wenches
  Cam skelpan up the way.   hurrying
Twa had manteeles o' dolefu' black,   capes
  But ane wi' lyart lining;   grey
The third, that gaed a wee a-back,   a little in the rear
  Was in the fashion shining
        Fu' gay that day.

III

The *twa* appear'd like sisters twin,
20 In feature, form an' claes;   clothes
Their visage wither'd, lang an' thin,
  An' sour as ony slaes: sloes

The *third* cam up, hap-step-an'-loup,   hop-step-and-jump
   As light as ony lambie,   little lamb
An' wi' a curchie low did stoop,   curtsy
   As soon as e'er she saw me,
       Fu' kind that day.

IV

Wi' bonnet aff, quoth I, 'Sweet lass,
   I think ye seem to ken me;
30 I'm sure I've seen that bonie face,
   But yet I canna name ye.'
Quo' she, an' laughan as she spak,   said, spoke
   An' taks me by the han's,   hands
'Ye, for my sake, hae gien the feck   have given most
   Of a' the *ten comman's*   commandments
       A screed some day.'   tear/rent

V

'My name is FUN — your cronie dear,
   The nearest friend ye hae;
An' this is SUPERSTITION here,
40   An' that's HYPOCRISY.
I'm gaun to ********* *holy fair*,   [Mauchline]
   To spend an hour in daffin: frolic
Gin ye'll go there, yon runkl'd pair,   if, that wrinkled
   We will get famous laughin
       At them this day.'

VI

Quoth I, 'With a' my heart, I'll do't;
   I'll get my Sunday's sark on,   shirt
An' meet you on the holy spot;
   Faith, we'se hae fine remarkin!'   we'll, entertainment
50 Then I gaed hame at crowdie-time,   breakfast-time
   An' soon I made me ready;
For roads were clad, frae side to side,
   Wi' monie a wearie body,   person
       In droves that day.

VII

Here, farmers gash, in ridin graith,   *smart, habit*
  Gaed hoddan by their cotters;   *jogging, cottagers*
There, swankies young, in braw braid-claith,   *strapping lads,*
                                                      broadcloth
  Are springan owre the gutters.
The lasses, skelpan barefit, thrang,   *hurrying, barefoot,*
                                                      in a crowd
60   In silks an' scarlets glitter;
Wi' *sweet-milk cheese*, in monie a whang,   *thick slice*
  An' *farls*, bak'd wi' butter,   *bits of oaten*
                                                    bannock
     Fu' crump that day.   *'hard and brittle' (B)*

VIII

When by the *plate* we set our nose,
  Weel heaped up wi' ha'pence,
A greedy glowr *black-bonnet* throws,
  An' we maun draw our tippence.   *twopence*
Then in we go to see the show,
  On ev'ry side they're gath'ran;
70 Some carryan dails, some chairs an' stools,   *deal planks*
  An' some are busy bleth'ran   *chatting hard*
     Right loud that day.

IX

Here stands a shed to fend the showr's,
  An' screen our countra Gentry;
There, *racer Jess*, an' twathree wh—res,   *two or three*
  Are blinkan at the entry.
Here sits a raw o' tittlan jads,   *row, gossiping*
                                                    hussies
  Wi' heaving breasts an' bare neck;
An' there, a batch o' *Wabster lads*,   *weaver*
80 Blackguarding frae K*******ck   *roistering,*
                                                  [Kilmarnock]
     For *fun* this day.

X

Here, some are thinkan on their sins,
  An' some upo' their claes;
Ane curses feet that fyl'd his shins,   *fouled*
  Anither sighs an' prays:

On this hand sits an *Elect* swatch,   sample
   Wi' screw'd-up, grace-proud faces;   sanctimonious
On that, a set o' chaps, at watch,
   Thrang winkan on the lasses   throng
90   To *chairs* that day.

XI

O happy is that man, an' blest!
   Nae wonder that it pride him!
Whase ain dear lass, that he likes best,   own
   Comes clinkan down beside him!   sitting smartly
Wi' arm repos'd on the *chair-back*,
   He sweetly does compose him;
Which, by degrees, slips round her *neck*
   An's loof upon her *bosom*   palm
          Unkend that day.   unknown

XII

100 Now a' the congregation o'er
   Is silent expectation;
For ****** speels the holy door,   [Moodie] climbs
   Wi' tidings o' s—lv—t—n.
Should *Hornie*, as in ancient days,   Satan
   'Mang sons o' G— present him,
The vera sight o' ******'s face,
   To's ain *het hame* had sent him   hot home [Hell]
          Wi' fright that day.

XIII

Hear how he clears the points o' Faith
110   Wi' rattlin an' thumpin!
Now meekly calm, now wild in wrath,
   He's stampan, an' he's jumpan!
His lengthen'd chin, his turn'd up snout,
   His eldritch squeel an' gestures,   hideous
O how they fire the heart devout,
   Like *cantharidian* plaisters
          On sic a day!

XIV

But hark! the *tent* has chang'd its voice;   'field pulpit' (B)
   There's peace an' rest nae langer;
120 For a' the *real judges* rise,
   They canna sit for anger.
***** opens out his cauld harangues,   [Smith]
   On *practice* and on *morals*;
An' aff the *godly* pour in thrangs,
   To gie the jars an' barrels
      A lift that day.

XV

What signifies his barren shine,
   Of *moral pow'rs* an' *reason*?
His English style, an' gesture fine,
130   Are a' clean out o' season.
Like SOCRATES or ANTONINE,
   Or some auld pagan heathen,
The *moral man* he does define,
   But ne'er a word o' *faith* in
      That's right that day.

XVI

In guid time comes an antidote
   Against sic poosion'd nostrum;   poisoned remedy
For *******, frae the water-fit,   [Peebles], river-mouth
   Ascends the *holy rostrum*:
140 See, up he's got the word o' G—,
   An' meek an' mim has view'd it,   demure
While COMMON-SENSE has taen the road,
   An' aff, an' up the *Cowgate*
      Fast, fast that day.

XVII

Wee ****** niest the Guard relieves,   [Miller], next
   An' Orthodoxy raibles,   gabbles
Tho' in his heart he weel believes,
   An' thinks it auld wives' fables:

But faith! the birkie wants a *Manse*,   fellow
150   So, cannilie he hums them;   dextrously, takes
                                        them in
   Altho' his *carnal* Wit an' Sense
     Like hafflins-wise o'ercomes him   in half measure/
                                   partly
        At times that day.

XVIII

Now, butt an' ben, the Change-house fills,   in outer and inner
                                   room, tavern
   Wi' *yill-caup* Commentators: ale-cup
Here's crying out for bakes an' gills,   biscuits, drams
   An' there the pint-stowp clatters;   -measure
While thick an' thrang, an' loud an' lang,   closely engaged
                                   together
   Wi' *Logic*, an' wi' *Scripture*,
160   They raise a din, that, in the end,
     Is like to breed a rupture
        O' wrath that day.

XIX

Leeze me on Drink! it gies us mair   I'm all for
   Than either School or Colledge:
It kindles Wit, it waukens Lear,   wakens Learning
   It pangs us fou o' Knowledge.   stuffs, full
Be't *whisky-gill* or *penny-wheep*,   small beer
   Or ony stronger potion,
It never fails, on drinkin deep,
170   To kittle up our *notion*,   rouse, fancy
        By night or day.

XX

The lads an' lasses, blythely bent
   To mind baith *saul* an' *body*,   soul
Sit round the table, weel content,
   An' steer about the *toddy*.   whisky, hot water
                                 and sugar
On this ane's dress, an' that ane's leuk,   expression
   They're makin observations;
While some are cozie i' the neuk,   corner
   An' forming *assignations*
180   To meet some day.

XXI

But now the L—'s ain trumpet touts,   *blasts*
   Till a' the hills are rairan,   *roaring*
An' echoes back return the shouts;
   Black ****** is na spairan: *[Russel], sparing*
His piercin words, like Highlan swords,
   Divide the joints an' marrow;
His talk o' H—ll, whare devils dwell,
   Our vera *'Sauls does harrow'
      Wi' fright that day!

XXII

190 A vast, unbottom'd, boundless *Pit*,
   Fill'd fou o' *lowan brunstane*,   *blazing brimstone*
Whase raging flame, an' scorching heat,
   Wad melt the hardest whun-stane!   *whinstone*
The *half asleep* start up wi' fear,
   An' think they hear it roaran,
When presently it does appear,
   'Twas but some neebor *snoran*   *neighbour snoring*
      Asleep that day.

XXIII

'Twad be owre lang a tale to tell,
200   How monie stories past,
An' how they crouded to the yill,   *crowded, ale*
   When they were a' dismist:
How drink gaed round, in cogs an' caups,   *dishes, bowls*
   Amang the furms an' benches;   *forms*
An' *cheese* an' *bread*, frae women's laps,
   Was dealt about in lunches,
      An' dawds that day.   *hunks*

*Shakespeare's Hamlet

XXIV

In comes a gawsie, gash *Guidwife*,　　　jovial, neat matron
　　An' sits down by the fire,
210 Syne draws her *kebbuk* an' her knife;　　　then, cheese
　　The lasses they are shyer.
The auld *Guidmen*, about the *grace*,　　　husbands
　　Frae side to side they bother,
Till some ane by his bonnet lays,
　　An' gies them't, like a *tether*,　　　rope
　　　　Fu' lang that day.　　　very

XXV

Waesucks! for him that gets nae lass,　　　alas
　　Or lasses that hae naething!
Sma' need has he to say a grace,
220 　Or melvie his braw claithing!　　　'soil with meal' (B), clothing
O *Wives* be mindfu', ance yoursel,
　　How bonie lads ye wanted,
An' dinna, for a *kebbuck-heel*,　　　do not, heel of cheese
　　Let lasses be affronted
　　　　On sic a day!

XXVI

Now *Clinkumbell*, wi' rattlan tow,　　　bellringer, rope
　　Begins to jow an' croon;　　　toll and sound
Some swagger hame, the best they dow,　　　are able
　　Some wait the afternoon.
230 At slaps the billies halt a blink,　　　gaps in dyke, fellows
　　Till lasses strip their shoon:　　　shoes
Wi' *faith* an' *hope*, an' *love* an' *drink*,
　　They're a' in famous tune
　　　　For crack that day.　　　chat

XXVII

How monie hearts this day converts,
　　O' sinners and o' Lasses!
Their hearts o' stane, gin night are gane,　　　stone, by nightfall, gone
　　As saft as ony flesh is.　　　soft

There's some are fou o' *love divine*;
240   There's some are fou o' *brandy*;
An' monie jobs that day begin,   intrigues
    May end in *Houghmagandie*   fornication
        Some ither day.

ADDRESS TO THE DEIL

O Prince , O chief of many throned pow'rs,
That led th'embattl'd Seraphim to war —

                Milton

O THOU, whatever title suit thee!
Auld Hornie, Satan, Nick, or Clootie,   Cloven-hoof
Wha in yon cavern grim an' sootie,
    Clos'd under hatches,
Spairges about the brunstane cootie,   bespatters, brimstone tub
    To scaud poor wretches!   scald

Hear me, *auld Hangie*, for a wee,   Hangman
An' let poor, *damned bodies* bee;
I'm sure sma' pleasure it can gie,
10   Ev'n to a *deil*,   devil
To skelp an' scaud poor dogs like me,   smack
    An' hear us squeel!

Great is thy pow'r, an' great thy fame;
Far kend an' noted is thy name;
An' tho' yon *lowan heugh's* thy hame,   blazing pit
    Thou travels far;
An' faith! thou's neither lag nor lame,   backward
    Nor blate nor scaur.   bashful, afraid

Whyles, ranging like a roaran lion,
20 For prey, a' holes an' corners tryin;
Whyles, on the strong-wing'd Tempest flyin,
      Tirlan the *kirks*;   uncovering,
                                          churches
Whyles, in the human bosom pryin,
      Unseen thou lurks.

I've heard my rev'rend *Graunie* say,   grandmother
In lanely glens ye like to stray;   lonely
Or where auld, ruin'd castles, gray,
      Nod to the moon,
Ye fright the nightly wand'rer's way,
30   Wi' eldritch croon.   unearthly moan

When twilight did my *Graunie* summon,
To say her pray'rs, douse, honest woman!   sober
Aft 'yont the dyke she's heard you bumman,   behind, wall,
                                      humming
      Wi' eerie drone;
Or, rustling, thro' the boortries coman,   elder trees
      Wi' heavy groan.

Ae dreary, windy, winter night,
The stars shot down wi' sklentan light,   slanting
Wi' you, *mysel*, I gat a fright,
40   Ayont the lough;   beyond, loch
Ye, like a *rash-buss*, stood in sight,   clump of rushes
      Wi' waving sugh.   sound of wind

The cudgel in my neive did shake,   fist
Each bristl'd hair stood like a stake,
When wi' an eldritch, stoor *quaick, quaick*,   harsh
      Amang the springs,
Awa ye squatter'd like a *drake*,   'flutter in water' (B)
      On whistling wings.

Let *Warlocks* grim, an' wither'd *Hags*,
50 Tell how wi' you on ragweed nags,   ragwort
They skim the muirs an' dizzy crags,   moors

Wi' wicked speed;
And in kirk-yards renew their leagues,
　　Owre howcket dead.   exhumed

Thence, countra wives, wi' toil an' pain,
May plunge an' plunge the *kirn* in vain;   churn
For Oh! the yellow treasure's taen
　　By witching skill;
60   An' dawtet, twal-pint *Hawkie's* gane   spoiled, twelve-,
　　　　As yell's the Bill.   cow
　　　　　　　　　　　　　　　　　　　　milkless as, bull

Thence, mystic knots mak great abuse,
On *Young-Guidmen*, fond, keen an' croose;   -husbands,
confident
When the best *wark-lume* i' the house,   work-loom
　　By cantraip wit,   magic
Is instant made no worth a louse,
　　　　Just at the bit.   critical moment

When thowes dissolve the snawy hoord,   thaws, snowy drift
An' float the jinglan icy boord,   (on), cracking,
surface
Then, *Water-kelpies* haunt the foord,   waterhorse
demons, ford
70   By your direction,
An' nighted Trav'llers are allur'd
　　　　To their destruction.

An' aft your moss-traversing *Spunkies*   wills o' the wisp
Decoy the wight that late an' drunk is:
The bleezan, curst, mischievous monkies   blazing
　　Delude his eyes,
Till in some miry slough he sunk is,
　　　　Ne'er mair to rise.

When MASONS' mystic *word* an' *grip*,
80   In storms an' tempests raise you up,
Some cock or cat, your rage maun stop,
　　Or, strange to tell!
The *youngest Brother* ye wad whip
　　　　Aff straught to *H—ll*.   straight

Lang syne in EDEN's bonie yard,   long ago, garden
When youthfu' lovers first were pair'd,
An' all the Soul of Love they shar'd,
     The raptur'd hour,
Sweet on the fragrant, flow'ry swaird,   sward
90   In shady bow'r.

Then you, ye auld, snick-drawing dog!   latch-
Ye cam to Paradise incog,   unknown
An' play'd on man a cursed brogue,   trick
     (Black be your fa'!)
An' gied the infant warld a shog,   world, shock
     'Maist ruin'd a'.

D'ye mind that day, when in a bizz,   remember, stir
Wi' reeket duds, an' reestet gizz,   smoky clothes, 'cured' wig
Ye did present your smoutie phiz,   ugly face
100   'Mang better folk,
An' sklented on the *man of Uzz*,   directed aslant
     Your spitefu' joke?

An how ye gat him i' your thrall,
An' brak him out o' house an' hal',
While scabs an' botches did him gall,   'angry tumours' (B)
     Wi' bitter claw,   scratching
An' lows'd his ill-tongu'd, wicked *Scawl*   loosed, abusive woman
     Was warst ava?   worst of all

But a' your doings to rehearse,
110 Your wily snares an' fechtin fierce,   fighting
Sin' that day *MICHAEL did you pierce,
     Down to this time,
Wad ding a' *Lallan* tongue, or *Erse*,   weary, Lowland, Gaelic
     In Prose or Rhyme.

*Vide Milton, Book 6th

An' now, auld *Cloots*, I ken ye're thinkan,
A certain *Bardie's* rantin, drinkin,   poet
Some luckless hour will send him linkan,   going briskly
  To your black pit;
But faith! he'll turn a corner jinkan,   side-stepping
120   An' cheat you yet.

But fare-you-weel, auld *Nickie-ben*!
O wad ye tak a thought an' men'!   and mend
Ye aiblins might – I dinna ken –   perhaps
  Still hae a *stake* –   chance
I'm wae to think upo' yon den,   unhappy
  Ev'n for your sake!

The Death and Dying Words of
POOR MAILIE,
The Author's Only Pet Yowe,
An Unco Mournfu' Tale

As MAILIE, an' her lambs thegither,
Was ae day nibbling on the tether,
Upon her cloot she coost a hitch,   hoof, cast
An' owre she warsl'd in the ditch: struggled
There, groaning, dying, she did ly,
When *Hughoc he cam doytan by.   blundering

 Wi' glowrin een, an' lifted han's,   eyes, hands
Poor *Hughoc* like a statue stan's;
He saw her days were near hand ended,   almost
10 But, waes my heart! he could na mend it!   woe is
He gaped wide, but naething spak,   spoke
At length poor *Mailie* silence brak.   broke

*A neibor herd-callan.

'O thou, whase lamentable face
Appears to mourn my woefu' case!
My *dying words* attentive hear,
An' bear them to my *Master* dear.

'Tell him, if e'er again he keep
As muckle gear as buy a *sheep*,   money
O, bid him never tye them mair,
20 Wi' wicked strings o' hemp or hair!
But ca them out to park or hill,
An' let them wander at their will:
So, may his flock increase an' grow
To *scores* o' lambs, an' *packs* of woo'!   wool

'Tell him, he was a Master kin',   kindly
An' ay was guid to me an' mine;
An' now my *dying* charge I gie him,
My helpless *lambs*, I trust them wi' him.

'O, bid him save their harmless lives,
30 Frae dogs an' tods, an' butchers' knives!   foxes
But gie them guid *cow-milk* their fill,
Till they be fit to fend themsel;
An' tent them duely, e'en an' morn,   tend
Wi' taets o' *hay* an' ripps o' *corn*.   tufts, handfuls

'An' may they never learn the gaets,   ways
Of ither vile, wanrestfu' *Pets*!   restless
To slink thro' slaps, an' reave an' steal,   gaps, plunder
At stacks o' pease, or stocks o' kail.   green kale
So may they, like their great *forbears*,
40 For monie a year come thro' the sheers:
So *wives* will gie them bits o' bread,
An' *bairns* greet for them when they're dead.   weep

'My poor *toop-lamb*, my son an' heir,   ram-
O, bid him breed him up wi' care!
An' if he live to be a beast,
To pit some havins in his breast!   put, sense

An' warn him ay at riding time,
To stay content wi' *yowes* at hame;
An' no to rin an' wear his cloots,   run, hooves
50 Like ither menseless, graceless brutes.   ill-bred, senseless

   'An' niest my *yowie*, silly thing,   next, young ewe
Gude keep thee frae a *tether string*!
O, may thou ne'er forgather up,
Wi' onie blastet, moorlan *toop*;   accursed, ram
But ay keep mind to moop an' mell,   nibble, mix
Wi' sheep o' credit like thysel!

   'And now, *my bairns*, wi' my last breath,
I lea'e my blessin wi' you baith:
An' when ye think upo' your Mither,   mother
60 Mind to be kind to ane anither.   remember

   'Now, honest Hughoc, dinna fail,   don't
To tell my Master a' my tale;
An' bid him burn this cursed *tether*,
An' for thy pains thou'se get my blather.'   you will, bladder

   This said, poor *Mailie* turn'd her head,
An' clos'd her een amang the dead!

POOR MAILIE'S ELEGY

LAMENT in rhyme, lament in prose,
Wi' saut tears trickling down your nose;   salt
Our *Bardie's* fate is at a close,   poet's
    Past a' remead!   cure
The last, sad cape-stane of his woes;   coping-stone
    Poor *Mailie's* dead!

It's no the loss o' warl's gear,   *worldly property*
That could sae bitter draw the tear,
Or make our *Bardie*, dowie, wear   *sad*
10   The mourning weed:
He's lost a friend and neebor dear,   *neighbour*
    In *Mailie* dead.

Thro' a' the town she trotted by him;   *village/farm*
A lang half-mile she could descry him;
Wi' kindly bleat, when she did spy him,
    She ran wi' speed:
A friend mair faithfu' ne'er came nigh him,
    Than *Mailie* dead.

I wat she was a *sheep* o' sense,   *know*
20 An' could behave hersel wi' mense: *discretion*
I'll say't, she never brak a fence,   *broke*
    Thro' thievish greed.
Our *Bardie*, lanely, keeps the spence,   *lonely, inner room*
    Sin' *Mailie's* dead.

Or, if he wanders up the howe,   *valley*
Her living image in *her yowe*,   *ewe*
Comes bleating till him, owre the knowe,   *to*
    For bits o' bread;
An' down the briny pearls rowe   *roll*
30   For *Mailie* dead.

She was nae get o' moorlan tips,   *offspring, tups*
Wi' tauted ket, an' hairy hips;   *matted fleece*
For her forbears were brought in ships,
    Frae 'yont the TWEED: *beyond*
A bonier *fleesh* ne'er cross'd the clips   *fleece, shears*
    Than *Mailie's* dead.

Wae worth that man wha first did shape,   *woe to*
That vile, wanchancie thing – *a raep*!   *unlucky, rope*
It maks guid fellows girn an' gape,   *'twist the features in rage' (B)*

40   Wi' chokin dread;
    An' *Robins's* bonnet wave wi' crape
       For *Mailie* dead.

O, a' ye *Bards* on bonie DOON!
An' wha on AIRE your chanters tune!
Come, join the melancholious croon   moan
      O' *Robin*'s reed!
His heart will never get aboon!   above
      His *Mailie's* dead!

TO J. S****

Friendship, mysterious cement of the soul!
Sweet'ner of Life, and solder of Society!
I owe thee much ——

                Blair

DEAR S****, the sleest, pawkie thief,   cleverest, humorous
That e'er attempted stealth or rief,   plunder
Ye surely hae some warlock-breef   charm/wizard-spell
      Owre human hearts;
For ne'er a bosom yet was prief   proof
      Against your arts.

For me, I swear by sun an' moon,
And ev'ry star that blinks aboon,   above
Ye've cost me twenty pair o' shoon   shoes
10   Just gaun to see you;
And ev'ry ither pair that's done,
      Mair taen I'm wi' you.

That auld, capricious carlin, *Nature*,   old woman
To mak amends for scrimpet stature,   stunted
She's turn'd you off, a human-creature

On her *first* plan,
And in her freaks, on ev'ry feature,
She's wrote, *the Man*.

20 Just now I've taen the fit o' rhyme,
My barmie noddle's working prime,   yeasty brain
My fancy yerket up sublime   stirred
    Wi' hasty summon:
Hae ye a leisure-moment's time
      To hear what's coming?

Some rhyme a neebor's name to lash;   neighbour
Some rhyme, (vain thought!) for needfu' cash;
Some rhyme to court the countra clash, invite, talk
    An' raise a din;
For me, an *aim* I never fash;   bother about
30   I rhyme for *fun*.

The star that rules my luckless lot,
Has fated me the russet coat,   poor man's rural wear
An' damn'd my fortune to the groat;   small coin
    But, in requit,   by way of compensation
Has blest me with a *random-shot*
      O' countra wit.

This while my notion's taen a sklent,   slant/turn
To try my fate in guid, black *prent*; print
But still the mair I'm that way bent,
40   Something cries, 'hoolie!   'take leisure, stop!' (B)
I red you, honest man, tak tent!   advise, take care
      Ye'll shaw your folly.   show

'There's ither Poets, much your betters,
Far seen in *Greek*, deep men o' *letters*, well-versed
Hae thought they had ensur'd their debtors, insured as
    A' future ages;
Now moths deform in shapeless tatters,
      Their unknown pages.'

Then farewell hopes of Laurel-boughs,
50   To garland my poetic brows!
Henceforth, I'll rove where busy ploughs
        Are whistling thrang,   busily
An' teach the lanely heights an' howes   lonely, hollows
        My rustic sang.

I'll wander on with tentless heed,   careless
How never-halting moments speed,
Till fate shall snap the brittle thread;
        Then, all unknown,
I'll lay me with th'*inglorious dead*,
60   Forgot and gone!

But why, o' Death, begin a tale?
Just now we're living sound an' hale;
Then top and maintop croud the sail,   crowd
        Heave *Care* o'er-side!
And large, before Enjoyment's gale,
        Let's tak the tide.

This life, sae far's I understand,   so far as
Is a' enchanted fairy-land;
Where Pleasure is the Magic-wand,
70   That, wielded right,
Maks Hours like Minutes, hand in hand,
        Dance by fu' light.   full

The *magic-wand* then let us wield;
For, ance that five an' forty's speel'd,   climbed
See, crazy, weary, joyless Eild,   Old Age
        Wi' wrinkl'd face,
Comes hostan, hirplan owre the field,   coughing, limping
        Wi' creeping pace.

When ance *life's day* draws near the gloamin,   twilight
80   Then fareweel vacant, careless roamin;
An' fareweel chearfu' tankards foamin,

An' social noise;
An' fareweel dear, deluding woman,
  The joy of joys!

O *Life*! how pleasant in thy morning,
Young Fancy's rays the hills adorning!
Cold-pausing Caution's lesson scorning,
  We frisk away,
Like school-boys, at th'expected warning,
90   To joy and play.

We wander there, we wander here,
We eye the *rose* upon the brier,
Unmindful that the *thorn* is near,
  Among the leaves;
And tho' the puny wound appear,
  Short while it grieves.

Some, lucky, find a flow'ry spot,
For which they never toil'd nor swat;   sweated
They drink the *sweet* and eat the *fat*,
100 But care or pain;   without
And haply, eye the barren hut,
  With high disdain.

With steady aim, Some Fortune chase;
Keen hope does ev'ry sinew brace;
Thro' fair, thro' foul, they urge the race,
  And seize the prey:
Then canie, in some cozie place,   cautious,
  They close the *day*.   comfortable

And others, like your humble servan',
110 *Poor wights*! nae rules nor roads observin; fellows
To right or left, eternal swervin,
  They zig-zag on;
Till curst with Age, obscure an' starvin,
  They aften groan.

Alas! what bitter toil an' straining —
But truce with peevish, poor complaining!
Is Fortune's fickle *Luna* waning?   Moon
      E'en let her gang!
Beneath what light she has remaining,
120   Let's sing our Sang.

My pen I here fling to the door,
And kneel, 'Ye *Pow'rs*', and warm implore,
'Tho' I should wander *Terra* o'er,   Earth
      In all her climes,
Grant me but this, I ask no more,
      Ay rowth o' rhymes.   plenty

'Gie dreeping roasts to *countra Lairds*,   dripping
Till icicles hing frae their beards;   hang
Gie fine braw claes to fine *Life-guards*,   clothes
130   And *Maids of Honor*;
And yill an' whisky gie to *Cairds*,   ale, tinkers
      Until they sconner.   feel disgust

'A *Title*, DEMPSTER merits it;
A *Garter* gie to WILLIE PIT;
Gie Wealth to some be-ledger'd Cit,   townsman
      In cent per cent;
But give me real, sterling Wit,
      And I'm content.

'While ye are pleas'd to keep me hale,   healthy
140 I'll sit down o'er my scanty meal,
Be't *water-brose*, or *muslin-kail*,   -porridge, meatless broth
      Wi' chearfu' face,
As lang's the Muses dinna fail
      To say the grace.'

An anxious e'e I never throws   eye
Behint my lug, or by my nose;   ear
I jouk beneath Misfortune's blows   dodge

As weel's I may,
Sworn foe to *sorrow, care,* and *prose,*
150   I rhyme away.

O ye, douse folk, that live by rule,   sedate
Grave, tideless-blooded, calm and cool,
Compar'd wi' you – O fool! fool! fool!
        How much unlike!
Your hearts are just a standing pool,
        Your lives, a dyke!   stone wall

Nae hare-brain'd, sentimental traces,
In your unletter'd, nameless faces!
In *arioso* trills and graces
160   Ye never stray,
But *gravissimo,* solemn basses
        Ye hum away.

Ye are sae *grave,* nae doubt ye're *wise;*
Nae ferly tho' ye do despise   wonder
The hairum-scairum, ram-stam boys,   wild, reckless
        The rambling squad:
I see ye upward cast your eyes –
        – Ye ken the road –

Whilst I – but I shall haud me there –   hold
170 Wi' you I'll scarce gang *ony where –*
Then *Jamie,* I shall say nae mair,
        But quat my sang,   end
Content *with* YOU to mak a *pair,*
        Whare'er I gang.

A DREAM

Thoughts, words and deeds, the Statute blames with reason;
But surely Dreams were ne'er indicted Treason.

On Reading, in the Public Papers, the Laureate's Ode, with the other
Parade of June 4th, 1786, the Author was no sooner dropt asleep, than
he imagined himself transported to the Birthday Levee; and, in his
dreaming Fancy, made the following Address.

I

GUID-MORNIN to your MAJESTY!
    May heaven augment your blisses,
On ev'ry new *Birth-day* ye see,
    A humble Bardie wishes!   *poet*
My Bardship here, at your Levee,
    On sic a day as this is,
Is sure an uncouth sight to see,
    Amang thae Birth-day dresses   *those*
        Sae fine this day.

II

10   I see ye're complimented thrang,   *busily*
    By many a *lord* an' *lady*;
'God save the King' 's a cuckoo sang
    That's unco easy said ay:
The *Poets* too, a venal gang,
    Wi' rhymes weel-turn'd an' ready,
Wad gar you trow ye ne'er do wrang,   *make, believe,*
    But ay unerring steady,   *wrong*
        On sic a day.

III

For me! before a Monarch's face,
20   Ev'n *there* I winna flatter;   *will not*
For neither Pension, Post, nor Place,
    Am I your humble debtor:

So, nae reflection on YOUR GRACE,
 Your Kingship to bespatter;
There's monie *waur* been o' the Race,   worse
 And aiblins *ane* been better   perhaps one
    Than You this day.   [Charles Stewart]

IV

'Tis very true, my sovereign King,
 My skill may weel be doubted;
30 But *Facts* are cheels that winna ding,   fellows, will not be
 An' downa be disputed: shifted
Your *royal nest*, beneath *Your* wing,   cannot
 Is e'en right reft an' clouted,   torn, patched
And now the third part o' the string,
 An' less, will gang about it
    Than did ae day.

V

Far be't frae me that I aspire
 To blame your Legislation,
Or say, ye wisdom want, or fire,
40 To rule this mighty nation;
But faith! I muckle doubt, my SIRE,
 Ye've trusted 'Ministration,
To chaps, wha, in a *barn* or *byre*,   cow-shed
 Wad better fill'd their station
    Than *courts* yon day.

VI

And now Ye've gien auld *Britain* peace,
 Her broken shins to plaister;   plaster
Your sair taxation does her fleece,
 Till she has scarce a tester: sixpence
50 For me, thank God, my life's a *lease*,
 Nae *bargain* wearing faster,
Or faith! I fear, that, wi' the geese,
 I shortly boost to pasture   must
    I' the craft some day.   croft

VII

I'm no mistrusting *Willie Pit*,
  When taxes he enlarges,
(An' *Will's* a true guid fallow's get   fellow's son
  A Name not Envy spairges)   bespatters
That he intends to pay your *debt*,
60   An' lessen a' your *charges*;
  But, G—d-sake! let nae *saving-fit*
    Abridge your bonie *Barges*
        An' *Boats* this day.

VIII

Adieu, my LIEGE! may Freedom geck   exult
  Beneath your high protection;
An' may Ye rax Corruption's neck,   wring
  And gie her for dissection!
But since I'm here, I'll no neglect,
  In loyal, true affection,
70 To pay your QUEEN, with due respect,
    My fealty an' subjection
        This great Birth-day.

IX

Hail, *Majesty most Excellent*!
  While Nobles strive to please Ye,
Will Ye accept a Compliment,
  A simple Bardie gies Ye?
Thae bonie Bairntime, Heav'n has lent,   offspring
  Still higher may they heeze Ye   lift
In bliss, till Fate some day is sent,
80   For ever to release Ye
        Frae Care that day.

X

For you, young Potentate o' W—,   [Wales]
  I tell your *Highness* fairly,
Down Pleasure's stream, wi' swelling sails,
  I'm tauld ye're driving rarely;   told

But some day ye may gnaw your nails,
   An' curse your folly sairly,   *sorely*
That e'er ye brak Diana's *pales*,   *broke*
   Or rattl'd dice wi' *Charlie*
90   By night or day.

XI

Yet aft a ragged *Cowte's* been known,   *colt*
   To mak a noble *Aiver*;   *'old horse'* (B)
So, ye may dousely fill a Throne,   *decorously*
   For a' their clish-ma-claver: *gossip*
There, Him at *Agincourt* wha shone,
   Few better were or braver;
And yet, wi' funny, queer *Sir *John*,
   He was an unco shaver   *joker*
         For monie a day.

XII

100 For you, right rev'rend O——,   *[Osnaburg]*
   Nane sets the *lawn-sleeve* sweeter, *becomes*
Altho' a ribban at your lug   *ear*
   Wad been a dress compleater:
As ye disown yon paughty dog,   *insolent*
   That *bears* the Keys of Peter,
Then swith! an' get a *wife* to hug,   *quickly*
   Or trouth! ye'll stain the *Mitre*
         Some luckless day.

XIII

Young, royal TARRY-BREEKS, I learn, *'tar-trousers'*
110 Ye've lately come athwart her;
A glorious †*Galley*, stem and stern,
   Weel rigg'd for *Venus barter*;
But first hang out that she'll discern
   Your *hymeneal Charter*,

---

*Sir John Falstaff, Vide Shakespeare.

†Alluding to the Newspaper account of a certain royal Sailor's Amour.

Then heave aboard your *grapple airn*,   grappling-iron
  An', large upon her *quarter*,   quarter-deck
      Come full that day.

XIV

Ye lastly, bonie blossoms a',
  Ye *royal Lasses* dainty,
120 Heav'n mak you guid as weel as braw,
  An' gie you *lads* a plenty:
But sneer na *British-boys* awa;
  For King's are unco scant ay,
An' German-Gentles are but *sma'*,   -'great folks' (B)
  They're better just than *want ay*   none
      On onie day.

XV

God bless you a'! consider now,
  Ye're unco muckle dautet;   spoiled
But ere the *course* o' life be through,
130   It may be bitter sautet: salted
An' I hae seen their *coggie* fou,   dish, full
  That yet hae tarrow't at it,   who, 'murmured' (B)
But or the *day* was done, I trow,   before
  The laggen they hae clautet   bottom of dish, scraped
      Fu' clean that day.   very

THE VISION

DUAN FIRST*

THE sun had clos'd the *winter-day*,
The Curlers quat their roaring play,   *left*
And hunger'd Maukin taen her way   *the hare*
      To kail-yards green,   *kitchen-gardens*
While faithless snaws ilk step betray   *snows*
      Whare she has been.

The Thresher's weary *flingin-tree*,   *flail*
The lee-lang day had tir'd me;   *all day through*
And when the Day had clos'd his e'e,   *eye*
10   Far i' the West,
Ben i' the *Spence*, right pensivelie,   *'into the parlour' (B)*
      I gaed to rest.

There, lanely, by the ingle-cheek,   *lonely*
I sat and ey'd the spewing reek,   *smoke*
That fill'd, wi' hoast-provoking smeek,   *cough-, smoke*
      The auld, clay biggin;   *building*
And heard the restless rattons squeak   *rats*
      About the riggin.   *roof*

All in this mottie, misty clime,   *dusty*
20 I backward mus'd on wasted time,
How I had spent my *youthfu' prime*,
      An' done nae-thing,
But stringing blethers up in rhyme   *nonsense/idle talk*
      For fools to sing.

Had I to guid advice but harket,   *listened*
I might, by this, hae led a market,   *by now*
Or strutted in a Bank and clarket   *written up*

*Duan, a term of Ossian's for the different divisions of a digressive Poem. See his *Cath-Loda*, vol. 2 of McPherson's Translation.

                My *Cash-Account*;
While here, half-mad, half-fed, half-sarket,   half-clothed
                                                      ('-shirted')
30   Is a' th' amount.

I started, mutt'ring blockhead! coof!   fool!
And heav'd on high my wauket loof,   calloused palm
To swear by a' yon starry roof,
                Or some rash aith,   oath
That I, henceforth, would be *rhyme-proof*
                Till my last breath –

When click! the *string* the *snick* did draw;   latch
And jee! the door gaed to the wa';   with a swing
And by my ingle-lowe I saw,   firelight
40   Now bleezan bright,   blazing
A tight, outlandish *Hizzie*, braw,   shapely, wench
                Come full in sight.

Ye need na doubt, I held my whisht;   kept silent
The infant aith, half-form'd, was crusht;
I glowr'd as eerie's I'd been dusht,   'pushed by a ram'
                In some wild glen;   (B)
When sweet, like *modest Worth*, she blusht,
                And stepped ben.   within

Green, slender, leaf-clad *Holly-boughs*
50 Were twisted, gracefu', round her brows,
I took her for some SCOTTISH MUSE,
                By that same token;
And come to stop those reckless vows,
                Would soon been broken.

A 'hare-brain'd, sentimental trace'
Was strongly marked in her face;
A wildly-witty, rustic grace
                Shone full upon her;
Her *eye*, ev'n turn'd on empty space,
60   Beam'd keen with *Honor*.

Down flow'd her robe, a *tartan* sheen,
Till half a leg was scrimply seen;   barely
And such a *leg*! my BESS, I ween,
      Could only peer it;   equal
Sae straught, sae taper, tight and clean,   straight, shapely
      Nane else came near it.

Her *Mantle* large, of greenish hue,
My gazing wonder chiefly drew;
Deep *lights* and *shades*, bold-mingling, threw
70   A lustre grand;
And seem'd, to my astonish'd view,
      A *well-known* Land.

Here, rivers in the sea were lost;
There, mountains to the skies were tost:
Here, tumbling billows mark'd the coast,
      With surging foam;
There, distant shone, *Art's* lofty boast,
      The lordly dome.

Here, DOON pour'd down his far-fetch'd floods;
80 There, well-fed IRWINE stately thuds:
Auld, hermit AIRE staw thro' his woods,   crept
      On to the shore;
And many a lesser torrent scuds,
      With seeming roar.

Low, in a sandy valley spread,
An ancient BOROUGH rear'd her head;
Still, as in *Scottish Story* read,
      She boasts a *Race*,
To ev'ry nobler virtue bred,
90   And polish'd grace.

DUAN SECOND

With musing-deep, astonish'd stare,
I view'd the heavenly-seeming *Fair*;
A whisp'ring *throb* did witness bear
          Of kindred sweet,
When with an elder Sister's air
          She did me greet.

'All hail! *my own* inspired Bard!
In me thy native Muse regard!
Nor longer mourn thy fate is hard,
100   Thus poorly low!
I come to give thee such *reward*,
          As *we* bestow.

'Know, the great *Genius* of this Land,
Has many a light, aerial band,
Who, all beneath his high command,
          Harmoniously,
As *Arts* or *Arms* they understand,
          Their labors ply.

'They SCOTIA'S Race among them share;
110 Some fire the *Sodger* on to dare;   soldier
Some rouse the *Patriot* up to bare
          Corruption's heart:
Some teach the *Bard*, a darling care,
          The tuneful Art.

''Mong swelling floods of reeking gore,
They ardent, kindling spirits pour;
Or, mid the venal Senate's roar,
          They, sightless, stand,
To mend the honest *Patriot-lore*,
120   And grace the hand.

'Hence, FULLARTON, the brave and young;
Hence, DEMPSTER'S truth-prevailing tongue;
Hence, sweet harmonious BEATTIE sung
   His "Minstrel lays";
Or tore, with noble ardour stung,
   The *Sceptic's* bays.

'To lower Orders are assign'd,
The humbler ranks of Human-kind,
The rustic Bard, the lab'ring Hind,
130   The Artisan;
All chuse, as, various they're inclin'd,
   The various man.

'When yellow waves the heavy grain,
The threat'ning *Storm*, some, strongly, rein;
Some teach to meliorate the plain,
   With *tillage-skill*;
And some instruct the Shepherd-train,
   Blythe o'er the hill.

'Some hint the Lover's harmless wile;
140 Some grace the Maiden's artless smile;
Some soothe the Lab'rer's weary toil,
   For humble gains,
And make his *cottage-scenes* beguile
   His cares and pains.

'Some, bounded to a district-space,
Explore at large Man's *infant race*,
To mark the embryotic trace,
   Of *rustic Bard*;
And careful note each op'ning grace,
150   A guide and guard.

'*Of these am I* – COILA my name;
And this district as mine I claim,
Where once the *Campbells*, chiefs of fame,

Held ruling pow'r:
I mark'd thy embryo-tuneful flame,
      Thy natal hour.

'With future hope, I oft would gaze,
Fond, on thy little, early ways,
Thy rudely-caroll'd, chiming phrase,
160   In uncouth rhymes,
Fir'd at the simple, artless lays
      Of other times.

'I saw thee seek the sounding shore,
Delighted with the dashing roar;
Or when the *North* his fleecy store
      Drove thro' the sky,
I saw grim Nature's visage hoar,
      Struck thy young eye.

'Or when the deep-green-mantl'd Earth,
170   Warm-cherish'd ev'ry floweret's birth,
And joy and music pouring forth,
      In ev'ry grove,
I saw thee eye the gen'ral mirth
      With boundless love.

'When ripen'd fields, and azure skies,
Call'd forth the *Reaper's* rustling noise,
I saw thee leave their ev'ning joys,
      And lonely stalk,
To vent thy bosom's swelling rise,
180   In pensive walk.

'When *youthful Love*, warm-blushing, strong,
Keen-shivering shot thy nerves along,
Those accents, grateful to thy tongue,
      Th'adored *Name*,
I taught thee how to pour in song,
      To soothe thy flame.

'I saw thy pulse's maddening play,
Wild-send thee Pleasure's devious way,
Misled by Fancy's *meteor-ray*,
      By Passion driven;
But yet the *light* that led astray,
      Was *light* from Heaven.

'I taught thy manners-painting strains,
The *loves*, the *ways* of simple swains,
Till now, o'er all my wide domains,
      Thy fame extends;
And some, the pride of *Coila's* plains,
      Become thy friends.

'Thou canst not learn, nor I can show,
To paint with *Thomson's* landscape-glow;
Or wake the bosom-melting throe,
      With *Shenstone's* art;
Or pour, with *Gray*, the moving flow,
      Warm on the heart.

'Yet all beneath th'unrivall'd Rose,
The lowly Daisy sweetly blows;
Tho' large the forest's Monarch throws
      His army shade,
Yet green the juicy Hawthorn grows,
      Adown the glade.

'Then never murmur nor repine;
Strive in thy *humble sphere* to shine;
And trust me, not *Potosi's mine*,
      Nor *King's regard*,
Can give a bliss o'ermatching thine,
      A *rustic Bard*.

'To give my counsels all in one,
Thy *tuneful flame* still careful fan;
Preserve *the dignity of Man*,

220   With Soul erect;
     And trust, the UNIVERSAL PLAN
               Will all protect.

     '*And wear thou this*' – She solemn said,
     And bound the *Holly* round my head:
     The polish'd leaves, and berries red,
               Did rustling play;
     And, like a passing thought, she fled,
               In light away.

THE following POEM will, by many
Readers, be well enough understood; but, for
the sake of those who are unacquainted with
the manners and traditions of the country
where the scene is cast, Notes are added, to
give some account of the principal Charms
and Spells of that Night, so big with
Prophecy to the Peasantry in the West of
Scotland. The passion of prying into Futurity
makes a striking part of the history of
Human-nature, in its rude state, in all ages
and nations; and it may be some
entertainment to a philosophic mind, if any
such should honor the Author with a
perusal, to see the remains of it, among the
more unenlightened in our own.

HALLOWEEN*

Yes! let the Rich deride, the Proud disdain,
The simple pleasures of the lowly train;
To me more dear, congenial to my heart,
One native charm, than all the gloss of art.

Goldsmith

I

UPON that *night*, when Fairies light
   On *Cassilis Downans*† dance,
Or owre the lays, in splendid blaze,   leas
   On sprightly coursers prance;
Or for *Colean*, the rout is taen,

* Is thought to be a night when Witches, Devils, and other mischief-making
beings, are all abroad on their baneful, midnight errands: particularly, those
aerial people, the Fairies, are said, on that night, to hold a grand
Anniversary.

† Certain little, romantic, rocky, green hills in the neighbourhood of the
ancient seat of the Earls of Cassilis.

Beneath the moon's pale beams;
There, up the *Cove*,* to stray an' rove,
  Amang the rocks an' streams
    To sport that night.

II

10 Amang the bonie, winding banks,
    Where *Doon* rins, wimplin, clear,   *runs, winding*
  Where BRUCE† ance rul'd the martial ranks,
    An' shook his *Carrick* spear,
  Some merry, friendly, countra folks,
    Together did convene,
  To *burn* their nits, an' *pou* their stocks,   *nuts, pull*
    An' haud their *Halloween*   *hold/keep*
      Fu' blythe that night.   *very*

III

  The lasses feat, an' cleanly neat,   *spruce*
20   Mair braw than when they're fine;   *in their finery*
  Their faces blythe, fu' sweetly kythe,   *show*
    Hearts leal, an' warm, an' kin':   *loyal, kindly*
  The lads sae trig, wi' wooer-babs,   *trim, love-knots*
    Weel knotted on their garten,   *garters*
  Some unco blate, an' some wi' gabs,   *shy, chatter*
    Gar lasses hearts gang startin   *make*
      Whyles fast at night.

* A noted cavern near Colean-house, called the Cove of Colean; which, as well as Cassilis Downans, is famed, in country story, for being a favourite haunt of Fairies.

† The famous family of that name, the ancestors of ROBERT the great Deliverer of his country, were Earls of Carrick.

IV

Then, first an' foremost, thro' the kail,   greens
    Their *stocks** maun a' be sought ance;
30 They steek their een, an' grape an' wale,   shut, eyes, grope, choose
    For muckle anes, an' straught anes.   big, straight
Poor hav'rel *Will* fell aff the drift,   foolish, lost the way
    An' wander'd thro' the *Bow-kail*,   cabbage
An' pow't, for want o' better shift,   pulled, choice
    A *runt* was like a sow-tail   cabbage stalk [which]
        Sae bow't that night.   bent

V

Then, straught or crooked, yird or nane,   earth
    They roar an' cry a' throw'ther;   in confusion
The vera *wee-things*, toddlan, rin,
40   Wi' stocks out owre their shouther: shoulder
An' gif the *custock's* sweet or sour,   if, pith
    Wi' joctelegs they taste them;   pocket-knives
Syne coziely, aboon the door,   then snugly, above
    Wi' cannie care, they've plac'd them   knowing
        To lye that night.

---

* The first ceremony of Halloween, is pulling each a *Stock*, or plant of kail. They must go out, hand in hand, with eyes shut, and pull the first they meet with: its being big or little, straight or crooked, is prophetic of the size and shape of the grand object of all their Spells – the husband or wife. If any *yird*, or earth, stick to the root, that is *tocher*, or fortune; and the taste of the *custoc*, that is, the heart of the stem, is indicative of the natural temper and disposition. Lastly, the stems, or to give them their ordinary appellation, the *runts*, are placed somewhere above the head of the door; and the christian names of the people whom chance brings into the house, are, according to the priority of placing the *runts*, the names in question.

VI

The lasses staw frae 'mang them a',   stole
    To pou their *stalks o' corn*;*
But *Rab* slips out, an' jinks about,   dodges
    Behint the muckle thorn:
50 He grippet *Nelly* hard an' fast;
    Loud skirl'd a' the lasses;   screamed
But her *tap-pickle* maist was lost,   top-most grain
    When kiutlan in the *Fause-house*†   cuddling
      Wi' him that night.

VII

The auld Guidwife's weel-hoordet *nits*‡   mistress, hoarded
    Are round an' round divided,
An' monie lads an' lasses fates
    Are there that night decided:
Some kindle, couthie, side by side   sociably
60 An' *burn* thegither trimly;
Some start awa, wi' saucy pride,
    An' jump out owre the chimlie   fire-place
      Fu' high that night.

VIII

Jean slips in twa, wi' tentie e'e;   watchful, eye
    Wha 'twas, she wadna tell;
But this is *Jock*, an' this is *me*,
    She says in to hersel: whisper͡

---

* They go to the barn-yard, and pull each, at three several times, a stalk of Oats. If the third stalk wants the *top-pickle*, that is, the grain at the top of the stalk, the party in question will want the Maidenhead.

† When the corn is in a doubtful state, by being too green, or wet, the Stack-builder, by means of old timber, &c. makes a large apartment in his stack, with an opening in the side which is fairest exposed to the wind: this he calls a *Fause-house*.

‡ Burning the nuts is a favourite charm. They name the lad and lass to each particular nut, as they lay them in the fire; and according as they burn quietly together, or start from beside one another, the course and issue of the Courtship will be.

He bleez'd owre her, an' she owre him,   *blazed*
    As they wad never mair part,
70   Till fuff! he started up the lum,   *chimney*
    An' *Jean* had e'en a sair heart   *sore*
       To see't that night.

IX

Poor Willie, wi' his *bow-kail runt*,   *cabbage*
    Was *brunt* wi' primsie *Mallie*;   *burnt, prim*
An' *Mary*, nae doubt, took the drunt,   *huff*
    To be compar'd to *Willie*:
Mall's nit lap out, wi' pridefu' fling,   *leapt*
    An' her ain fit, it brunt it;   *own foot*
While *Willie* lap, an' swoor by *jing*,   *leapt, swore*
80   'Twas just the way he wanted
       To be that night.

X

Nell had the *Fause-house* in her min',
    She pits hersel an' *Rob* in;   *puts*
In loving bleeze they sweetly join,
    Till white in ase they're sobbin: *ashes*
Nell's heart was dancin at the view;
    She whisper'd *Rob* to leuk for't: *look*
Rob, stownlins, prie'd her bonie mou,   *by stealth, kissed, mouth*
    Fu' cozie in the neuk for't,   *corner*
90   Unseen that night.

XI

But *Merran* sat behint their backs,
    Her thoughts on *Andrew Bell*;
She lea'es them gashan at their cracks,   *leaves, gossiping, talk*
    An' slips out by hersel:

She thro' the yard the nearest taks,
   An' for the *kiln* she goes then,
An' darklins grapet for the *bauks*,   *in the dark, groped, beams*
   And in the *blue-clue** throws then,
      Right fear't that night.   *thoroughly afraid*

XII

100 An' ay she *win't*, an' ay she swat,   *wound, sweated*
   I wat she made nae jaukin;   *know, trifling*
Till something *held* within the *pat*,   *pot*
   Guid L—d! but she was quaukin!   *quaking*
But whether 'twas the *Deil* himsel,   *Devil*
   Or whether 'twas a *bauk-en'*,   *beam-end*
Or whether it was *Andrew Bell*,
   She did na wait on talkin
      To spier that night.   *ask*

XIII

Wee *Jenny* to her Graunie says,
110   'Will ye go wi' me Graunie?
I'll *eat the apple*† at the *glass*,
   I gat frae uncle Johnie:'
She fuff't her pipe wi' sic a lunt,   *puffed, smoke*
   In wrath she was sae vap'rin,   *vapouring*
She notic't na, an aizle brunt   *red ember, burned*
   Her braw, new, worset apron   *worsted*
      Out thro' that night.

---

* Whoever would, with success, try this spell, must strictly observe these directions. Steal out, all alone, to the *kiln*, and, darkling, throw into the *pot*, a clew of blue yarn: wind it in a new clew off the old one; and towards the latter end, something will hold the thread: demand, *wha hauds?* i.e. who holds? and answer will be returned from the kiln-pot, by naming the christian and sirname of your future Spouse.

† Take a candle, and go, alone, to a looking glass: eat an apple before it, and some traditions say you should comb your hair all the time: the face of your conjugal companion, *to be*, will be seen in the glass, as if peeping over your shoulder.

XIV

'Ye little Skelpie-limmer's-face! *naughty hussy's*
  I daur you try sic sportin, *dare*
120 As seek the *foul Thief* onie place,
    For him to spae your fortune: *tell*
  Nae doubt but ye may get a *sight*!
    Great cause ye hae to fear it;
  For monie a ane has gotten a fright,
    An liv'd an' di'd deleeret, *delirious*
      On sic a night.

XV

'Ae Hairst afore the *Sherra-moor*, *harvest, Sheriffmuir*
  I mind't as weel's yestreen, *remember, last night*
I was a gilpey then, I'm sure, *girl*
130 I was na past fyfteen:
  The Simmer had been cauld an' wat, *wet*
    An' *Stuff* was unco green; *grain*
  An' ay a rantan *Kirn* we gat, *rollicking harvest-home*
    An' just on *Halloween*
      It fell that night.

XVI

'Our *Stibble-rig* was *Rab M'Graen*, *chief harvester*
  A clever, sturdy fellow;
His Sin gat *Eppie Sim* wi' wean, *child*
  That liv'd in Achmacalla:
140 He gat *hemp-seed*,* I mind it weel,
    An' he made unco light o't;
But monie a day was *by himsel*, *beside himself*

---

* Steal out, unperceived, and sow a handful of hemp seed; harrowing it with any thing you can conveniently draw after you. Repeat, now and then, 'Hemp seed I saw thee, Hemp seed I saw thee; and him (or her) that is to be my true-love, come after me and pou thee.' Look over your left shoulder, and you will see the appearance of the person invoked, in the attitude of pulling hemp. Some traditions say, 'come after me and shaw thee,' that is, show thyself; in which case it simply appears. Others omit the harrowing, and say, 'come after me and harrow thee.'

He was sae sairly frighted   sorely
    That vera night.'

XVII

Then up gat fechtan *Jamie Fleck*,   fighting
    An' he swoor by his conscience,
That he could *saw hemp-seed* a peck;   sow
    For it was a' but nonsense:
The auld guidman raught down the pock,   master, reached,
                                                     bag
150   An' out a handfu' gied him;
Syne bad him slip frae 'mang the folk,   then
    Sometime when nae ane see'd him,
      An' try't that night.

XVIII

He marches thro' amang the stacks,
    Tho' he was something sturtan;   afraid
The *graip* he for a *harrow* taks,   dung-fork
    An' haurls at his curpan: drags, rump
And ev'ry now an' then, he says,
    'Hemp-seed I saw thee,   sow
160   An' her that is to be my lass,
    Come after me an' draw thee
      As fast this night.'

XIX

He whistl'd up *lord Lenox' march*,
    To keep his courage cheary;
Altho' his hair began to arch,
    He was sae fley'd an' eerie: badly scared
Till presently he hears a squeak,
    An' then a grane an' gruntle;   groan, grunt
He by his showther gae a keek,   shoulder, look
170   An' tumbl'd wi' a wintle   roll
      Out owre that night.

XX

He roar'd a horrid murder-shout,
  In dreadfu' desperation!
An' young an' auld come rinnan out,
  An' hear the sad narration:
He swoor 'twas hilchan *Jean M'Craw,*   limping
  Or crouchie *Merran Humphie,*   hump-backed
                Marion
Till stop! she trotted thro' them a';
  An' what was it but *Grumphie*   the pig
180   Asteer that night?   astir

XXI

Meg fain wad to the *Barn* gaen,   have gone
  To *winn three wechts o' naething;** winnow, sievefuls
But for to meet the Deil her lane,   all by herself
  She pat but little faith in: put
She gies the Herd a pickle nits,   shepherd, few
  An' twa red cheeket apples,
To watch, while for the *Barn* she sets,
  In hopes to see *Tam Kipples*
   That vera night.

XXII

190 She turns the key, wi' cannie thraw, cautious twist
  An' owre the threshold ventures;
But first on *Sawnie* gies a ca',   Sandy
  Syne bauldly in she enters: boldly
A *ratton* rattl'd up the wa',   rat
  An' she cry'd, L—d preserve her!

---

* This charm must likewise be performed, unperceived and alone. You go to the *barn*, and open both doors; taking them off the hinges, if possible; for there is danger, that the Being, about to appear, may shut the doors, and do you some mischief. Then take that instrument used in winnowing the corn, which, in our country-dialect, we call a *wecht*; and go thro' all the attitudes of letting down corn against the wind. Repeat it three times; and the third time, an apparition will pass thro' the barn, in at the windy door, and out at the other, having both the figure in question, and the appearance or retinue, marking the employment or station in life.

An' ran thro' midden-hole an' a',   gutter at foot of a
    An' pray'd wi' zeal and fervour,   dunghill
      Fu' fast that night.

XXIII

They hoy't out Will, wi' sair advice;   urged
200   They hecht him some fine braw ane;   promised
It chanc'd the *Stack* he *faddom't thrice*,*   timber-propped
    Was timmer-propt for thrawin: against bending
He taks a swirlie, auld *moss-oak*,   gnarled
    For some black, grousome *Carlin*;   old woman
An' loot a winze, an' drew a stroke,   let out an oath
    Till skin in blypes cam haurlin   shreds, peeling
      Aff's nieves that night.   fists

XXIV

A wanton widow *Leezie* was,
    As cantie as a kittlen;   lively, kitten
210   But Och! that night, among the shaws,   woods
    She gat a fearfu' settlin!
She thro' the whins, an' by the cairn,   gorse
    An' owre the hill gaed scrievin,   careering
Whare *three Lairds' lan's met at a burn*,†   lands
    To dip her *left sark-sleeve* in,   shirt-
      Was bent that night.

XXV

Whyles owre a linn the burnie plays,   waterfall, little
    As thro' the glen it wimpl't;   stream
Whyles round a rocky scar it strays;

---

* Take an opportunity of going, unnoticed, to a *Bear-stack*, and fathom it three times round. The last fathom of the last time, you will catch in your arms, the appearance of your future conjugal yoke-fellow.

† You go out, one or more, for this is a social spell, to a south-running spring or rivulet, where 'three Lairds' lands meet,' and dip your left shirt-sleeve. Go to bed in sight of a fire, and hang your wet sleeve before it to dry. Ly awake; and sometime near midnight, an apparition, having the exact figure of the grand object in question, will come and turn the sleeve, as if to dry the other side of it.

220	Whyles in a wiel it dimpl't;	eddy
	Whyles glitter'd to the nightly rays,	
	Wi' bickerin, dancin dazzle;	rushing
	Whyles cooket underneath the braes,	hid, hillsides
	Below the spreading hazle	
	Unseen that night.	

XXVI

	Amang the brachens, on the brae,	coarse ferns
	Between her an' the moon,	
	The Deil, or else an outler Quey,	young cow in the open
	Gat up an' gae a croon:	
230	Poor *Leezie's* heart maist lap the hool	leapt out of skin
	Near lav'rock-height she jumpet,	lark-height
	But mist a fit, an' in the *pool*,	foot
	Out owre the lugs she plumpet,	ears
	Wi' a plunge that night.	

XXVII

	In order, on the clean hearth-stane,	
	The *Luggies** three are ranged;	wooden dishes
	And ev'ry time great care is taen,	
	To see them duly changed:	
	Auld, uncle *John*, wha *wedlock's joys*,	
240	Sin' *Mar's-year* did desire,	1715 (Mar's Rising)
	Because he gat the toom dish thrice,	empty
	He heav'd them on the fire,	
	In wrath that night.	

* Take three dishes; put clean water in one, foul water in another, and leave the third empty: blindfold a person, and lead him to the hearth where the dishes are ranged; he (or she) dips the left hand: if by chance in the clean water, the future husband or wife will come to the bar of Matrimony, a Maid; if in the foul, a widow; if in the empty dish, it foretells, with equal certainty, no marriage at all. It is repeated three times; and every time the arrangement of the dishes is altered.

XXVIII

Wi' merry sangs, an' friendly cracks,
   I wat they did na weary;   *am sure*
And unco tales, an' funnie jokes,
   Their sports were cheap an' cheary:
Till *butter'd So'ns*,* wi' fragrant lunt,   *porridge, steam*
   Set a' their gabs a steerin;   *tongues, wagging*
250 Syne, wi' a social glass o' strunt,   *liquor*
   They parted aff careerin
      Fu' blythe that night.

THE AULD FARMER'S NEW-YEAR-MORNING SALUTATION TO HIS AULD MARE, MAGGIE, ON GIVING HER THE ACCUSTOMED RIPP OF CORN TO HANSEL IN THE NEW-YEAR

A *Guid New-year* I wish you Maggie!
Hae, there's a ripp to thy auld baggie: *fist of unthreshed corn, belly*
Tho' thou's howe-backet, now, an' knaggie,   *'sunk in the back' (B), bony*
    I've seen the day,
Thou could hae gaen like ony staggie   *colt*
    Out owre the lay.   *outfield*

Tho' now thou's dowie, stiff an' crazy,   *sickly, infirm*
An' thy auld hide as white's a daisie,
I've seen thee dappl't, sleek an' glaizie,   *glittering smooth like glass*
10   A bonie gray:
He should been tight that daur't to *raize* thee,   *capable, dared, provoke*
    Ance in a day.

---

* Sowens, with butter instead of milk to them, is always the *Halloween Supper*.

Thou ance was i' the foremost rank,
A *filly* buirdly, steeve an' swank,   *stately, strong, agile*
An' set weel down a shapely shank,
    As e'er tread yird;   *earth*
An' could hae flown out owre a stank,   *pool of standing water*
    Like onie bird.

It's now some nine-an'-twenty year,
20 Sin' thou was my *Guidfather's Meere*;   *father-in-law's mare*
He gied me thee, o' tocher clear,   *dowry*
    An' fifty mark;
Tho' it was sma', 'twas *weel-won* gear,   *property*
    An' thou was stark.   *strong*

When first I gaed to woo my *Jenny*,
Ye then was trottan wi' your Minnie: *mother*
Tho' ye was trickie, slee an' funnie,   *clever*
    Ye ne'er was donsie;   *ill-tempered*
But hamely, tawie, quiet an' cannie,   *'that handles quietly' (B)*
30   An' unco sonsie.   *tractable*

That *day*, ye pranc'd wi' muckle pride,
When ye bure hame my bonie *Bride*:   *bore*
An' sweet an' gracefu' she did ride
    Wi' maiden air!
KYLE-STEWART I could bragged wide,   *have challenged*
    For sic a *pair*.

Tho' now ye dow but hoyte and hoble,   *can only move clumsily*
An' wintle like a saumont-coble,   *roll, salmon-boat*
That day, ye was a jinker noble,   *high-spirited beast*
40   For heels an' win'!   *wind*
An' ran them till they a' did wauble   *wobble*
    Far, far behin'!

When thou an' I were young an' skiegh,   *mettlesome*
An' *Stable-meals* at Fairs were driegh,   *dreary*

How thou wad prance, an' snore, an' scriegh, *snort, neigh*
    An' tak the road!
Towns-bodies ran, an' stood abiegh, *town folk, at a shy distance*
    An' ca't thee mad.

When thou was corn't, an' I was mellow, *fed with corn*
50 We took the road ay like a Swallow:
At *Brooses* thou had ne'er a fellow, *wedding-races*
    For pith an' speed; *energy*
But ev'ry tail thou pay't them hollow, *beat*
    Whare'er thou gaed.

The sma', droot-rumpl't, hunter cattle, *with drooping haunches, beasts*
Might aiblins waur't thee for a brattle; *perhaps, beat, short race*
But *sax Scotch mile*, thou try't their mettle, *six*
    An' gart them whaizle: *made, wheeze*
Nae whip nor spur, but just a wattle *stick*
60   O' saugh or hazle. *willow*

Thou was a noble *Fittie-lan'*, *rear left plough horse*
As e'er in tug or tow was drawn! *leather or rope*
Aft thee an' I, in aught hours gaun, *eight*
    On guid March-weather,
Hae turn'd *sax rood* beside our han', *by ourselves*
    For days thegither.

Thou never braing't, an' fetch't, an' flisket, *drew unsteadily, gasped, fretted*
But thy *auld tail* thou wad hae whisket,
An' spread abreed thy weel-fill'd *brisket*, *abroad, breast*
70   Wi' pith an' pow'r,
Till sprittie knowes wad rair't an' risket *rushy, hillocks, roared, torn underfoot*
    An' slypet owre. *fallen*

When frosts lay lang, an' snaws were deep, *snows*
An' threaten'd *labor* back to keep,
I gied thy *cog* a wee-bit heap *dish*

Aboon the timmer; above, wooden edge
I ken'd my *Maggie* wad na sleep
    For that, or Simmer. without, before summer

In *cart* or *car* thou never reestet; stood restive
80 The steyest brae thou wad hae fac't it; stiffest hill
Thou never lap, an' sten't, an' breastet, leapt, reared, pulled forward
    Then stood to blaw; blow
But just thy step a wee thing hastet,
    Thou snoov't awa. went steadily on

My Pleugh is now thy *bairn-time* a'; plough-team, brood
Four gallant brutes, as e'er did draw;
Forby sax mae, I've sell't awa, beside six more, sold
    That thou hast nurst:
They drew me thretteen pund an' twa, thirteen
90   The vera warst. worst

Monie a sair daurk we twa hae wrought, hard day's labour
An' wi' the weary warl' fought! world
An' monie an' *anxious day*, I thought
    We wad be beat!
Yet here to *crazy Age* we're brought, infirm
    Wi' something yet.

An' think na, my auld, trusty *Servan'*,
That now perhaps thou's less deservin,
An' thy *auld days* may end in starvin', old age
100   For my last fow, firlot
A heapet *Stimpart*, I'll reserve ane measure of grain/quarter peck
    Laid by for you.

We've worn to crazy years thegither; lived
We'll toyte about wi' ane anither; totter/walk like old age
Wi' tentie care I'll flit thy tether, watchful, change
    To some hain'd rig, reserved field
Whare ye may nobly rax your leather, stretch, skin
    Wi' sma' fatigue.

THE COTTER'S SATURDAY NIGHT
INSCRIBED TO R. A****, Esq

Let not Ambition mock their useful toil,
  Their homely joys, and destiny obscure;
Nor Grandeur hear, with a disdainful smile,
  The short and simple annals of the Poor.

                                        Gray

I

MY lov'd, my honor'd, much respected friend,
  No mercenary Bard his homage pays;
With honest pride, I scorn each selfish end,
  My dearest meed, a friend's esteem and praise: reward
To you I sing, in simple Scottish lays,
  The *lowly train* in life's sequester'd scene;
The native feelings strong, the guileless ways,
  What A**** in a *Cottage* would have been;
Ah! tho' his worth unknown, far happier there
    I ween!   believe

II

10   November chill blaws loud wi' angry sugh;   blows, rushing sound
  The short'ning winter-day is near a close;
The miry beasts retreating frae the pleugh;   plough
  The black'ning trains o' craws to their repose: crows
The toil-worn COTTER frae his labor goes,   farm tenant/ cottager
  This night his weekly moil is at an end,   drudgery
Collects his *spades*, his *mattocks* and his *hoes*,
  Hoping the *morn* in ease and rest to spend,
And weary, o'er the moor, his course does
    homeward bend.

III

At length his lonely *Cot* appears in view,   cottage
20   Beneath the shelter of an aged tree;
The expectant *wee-things*, toddlan, stacher   stagger
    through

To meet their *Dad*, wi' flichterin noise   fluttering
   and glee.
His wee-bit ingle, blinkan bonilie,   little bit of fire
   His clean hearth-stane, his thrifty *Wifie's*   stone
   smile,
The *lisping infant*, prattling on his knee,
   Does a' his weary *kiaugh* and care beguile,   'carking anxiety' (B)
And makes him quite forget his labor and his toil.

IV

Belyve, the *elder bairns* come drapping in,   soon, dropping
   At *Service* out, amang the Farmers roun';
30   Some ca' the pleugh, some herd, some tentie rin   drive, careful, run
   A cannie errand to a neebor town: quiet, neighbouring
Their eldest hope, their *Jenny*, woman-grown,
   In youthfu' bloom, Love sparkling in her e'e,   eye
Comes hame, perhaps, to shew a braw new gown,   good-looking
   Or deposite her sair-won penny-fee,   hard-won
To help her *Parents* dear, if they in hardship be.

V

With joy unfeign'd, *brothers* and *sisters* meet,
   And each for other's weelfare kindly spiers: asks
The social hours, swift-wing'd, unnotic'd fleet;
40   Each tells the uncos that he sees or hears.   news/uncommon things
The Parents partial eye their hopeful years;
   Anticipation forward points the view;
The *Mother*, wi' her needle and her sheers,
   Gars auld claes look amaist as weel's the new;   makes, clothes
The *Father* mixes a' wi' admonition due.

VI

Their Master's and their Mistress's command,
   The *youngkers* a' are warned to obey;
And mind their labors wi' an eydent hand,   diligent
   And ne'er, tho' out of sight, to jauk or play: 'dally, trifle' (B)
50   'And O! be sure to fear the LORD alway!

And mind your *duty*, duly, morn and night!
Lest in temptation's path ye gang astray,
   Implore his *counsel* and assisting *might*:
They never sought in vain that sought the
      LORD aright.'

VII

But hark! a rap comes gently to the door;
   Jenny, wha kens the meaning o' the same,
Tells how a neebor lad came o'er the moor,
   To do some errands, and convoy her hame.   escort
The wily Mother sees the *conscious flame*
60   Sparkle in *Jenny's* e'e, and flush her cheek,
With heart-struck, anxious care enquires his
     name,
   While *Jenny* hafflins is afraid to speak;   half
Weel-pleas'd the Mother hears, it's nae wild,
     worthless *Rake*.

VIII

With kindly welcome, *Jenny* brings him ben;
   A *strappan youth*; he takes the Mother's eye;
Blythe *Jenny* sees the *visit's* no ill taen;
   The Father cracks of horses, pleughs and kye.   talks, cattle
The *Youngster's* artless heart o'erflows wi' joy,
   But blate and laithfu', scarce can weel behave;   shy, bashful
70   The Mother, wi' a woman's wiles, can spy
   What makes the *youth* sae bashfu' and sae grave;
Weel-pleas'd to think her *bairn's* respected like
     the lave.   rest

IX

O happy love! where love like this is found!
   O heart-felt raptures! bliss beyond compare!
I've paced much this weary, *mortal round*,
   And sage EXPERIENCE bids me this declare –
'If Heaven a draught of heavenly pleasure spare,
   One *cordial* in this melancholy *Vale*,

'Tis when a youthful, loving, *modest* Pair,
80   In other's arms, breathe out the tender tale,
Beneath the milk-white thorn that scents the
      ev'ning gale.'

X

Is there, in human form, that bears a heart--
    A Wretch! a Villain! lost to love and truth!
That can, with studied, sly, ensnaring art,
    Betray sweet Jenny's unsuspecting youth?
Curse on his perjur'd arts! dissembling smooth!
    Are *Honor, Virtue, Conscience*, all exil'd?
Is there no Pity, no relenting Ruth,
    Points to the Parents fondling o'er their Child?
90 Then paints the *ruin'd Maid*, and *their*
      distraction wild!

XI

But now the Supper crown their simple board,
    The healsome *Porritch*, chief of SCOTIA'S food: wholesome, porridge
The soupe their *only Hawkie* does afford, drink, cow
    That 'yont the hallan snugly chows her cood: beyond, partition, chews, cud
The *Dame* brings forth, in complimental mood,
    To grace the lad, her weel-hain'd kebbuck, fell, -kept, cheese, pungent
And aft he's prest, and aft he ca's it guid;
    The frugal *Wifie*, garrulous, will tell,
How 'twas a towmond auld, sin' Lint was i' twelvemonth, flax, flower
    the bell.

XII

100 The chearfu' Supper done, wi' serious face,
    They, round the ingle, form a circle wide;
The Sire turns o'er, with patriarchal grace,
    The big *ha'-Bible*, ance his *Father's* pride: hall-
His bonnet rev'rently is laid aside,
    His *lyart haffets* wearing thin and bare; grey, temples
Those strains that once did sweet in ZION
      glide,

He wales a portion with judicious care;   chooses
'*And let us worship GOD!*' he says with
          solemn air.

XIII

They chant their artless notes in simple guise;
110   They tune their *hearts*, by far the noblest aim:
Perhaps *Dundee's* wild warbling measures rise,
          Or plaintive *Martyrs*, worthy of the name;
Or noble *Elgin* beets the heaven-ward flame,   'adds fuel to' (B)
          The sweetest far of SCOTIA'S holy lays:
Compar'd with these, *Italian trills* are tame;
          The tickl'd ears no heart-felt raptures raise;
Nae unison hae they, with our CREATOR'S
          praise.

XIV

The priest-like Father reads the sacred page,
          How *Abram* was the Friend of GOD on high;
120   Or, *Moses* bade eternal warfare wage,
          With *Amalek's* ungracious progeny;
Or how the *royal Bard* did groaning lye,
          Beneath the stroke of Heaven's avenging ire;
Or *Job's* pathetic plaint, and wailing cry;
          Or rapt *Isaiah's* wild, seraphic fire;
Or other *Holy Seers* that tune the *sacred lyre*.

XV

Perhaps the *Christian Volume* is the theme,
          How *guiltless blood* for *guilty man* was shed;
How HE, who bore in heaven the second name,
130   Had not on Earth whereon to lay His head:
How His first *followers* and *servants* sped;
          The *Precepts sage* they wrote to many a land:
How *he*, who lone in *Patmos* banished,
          Saw in the sun a mighty angel stand;
And heard great *Bab'lon's* doom pronounc'd
          by Heaven's command.

XVI

Then kneeling down to HEAVEN'S ETERNAL KING,
    The *Saint*, the *Father*, and the *Husband* prays:
Hope 'springs exulting on triumphant wing,'*
    That *thus* they all shall meet in future days:
140 There, ever bask in *uncreated rays*,
    No more to sigh, or shed the bitter tear,
Together hymning their CREATOR'S praise,
    In *such society*, yet still more dear;
While circling Time moves round in an eternal
      sphere.

XVII

Compar'd with *this*, how poor Religion's pride,
    In all the pomp of *method*, and of *art*,
When men display to congregations wide,
    Devotion's ev'ry grace, except the *heart*!
The POWER, incens'd, the Pageant will desert,
150   The pompous strain, the sacerdotal stole;
But haply, in some *Cottage* far apart,
    May hear, well pleas'd, the language
      of the *Soul*;
And in His *Book of Life* the Inmates poor enroll.

XVIII

Then homeward all take off their sev'ral way;
    The youngling *Cottagers* retire to rest:
The Parent-pair their *secret homage* pay,
    And proffer up to Heaven the warm request,
That HE who stills the *raven's* clam'rous nest,
    And decks the *lily* fair in flow'ry pride,
160 Would, in the way *His Wisdom* sees the best,
    For *them* and for their *little ones* provide;
But chiefly, in their hearts with *Grace divine*
      preside.

* Pope's Windsor Forest.

XIX

From scenes like these, old SCOTIA'S grandeur
    springs,
    That makes her lov'd at home, rever'd abroad:
Princes and lords are but the breath of kings,
    'An honest man's the noblest work of GOD:'
And *certes*, in fair Virtue's heavenly road,
    The *Cottage* leaves the *Palace* far behind:
What is a lordling's pomp? a cumbrous load,
170   Disguising oft the *wretch* of human kind,
Studied in arts of Hell, in wickedness refin'd!

XX

O SCOTIA! my dear, my native soil!
    For whom my warmest wish to heaven is sent!
Long may thy hardy sons of *rustic toil*,
    Be blest with health, and peace, and sweet
        content!
And O may Heaven their simple lives prevent
    From *Luxury's* contagion, weak and vile!
Then howe'er *crowns* and *coronets* be rent,
    A *virtuous Populace* may rise the while,
180   And stand a wall of fire around their
        much-lov'd ISLE.

XXI

O THOU! who pour'd the *patriotic tide*,
    That stream'd thro' great, unhappy
        WALLACE' heart;
Who dar'd to, nobly, stem tyrannic pride,
    Or *nobly die*, the second glorious part:
(The Patriot's GOD, peculiarly thou art,
    His *friend, inspirer, guardian* and *reward*!)
O never, never SCOTIA'S realm desert,
    But still the *Patriot*, and the *Patriot-Bard*,
In bright succession raise, her *Ornament*
    and *Guard*!

TO A MOUSE,
On turning her up in her Nest,
with the Plough, November, 1785

WEE, sleeket, cowran, tim'rous *beastie*,   sleek, fearful, little creature
  O, what a panic's in thy breastie!   little breast
Thou need na start awa sae hasty,
      Wi' bickering brattle!   sound of scamper
I wad be laith to rin an' chase thee,   loath, run
      Wi' murd'ring *pattle*!   plough-staff

I'm truly sorry Man's dominion
Has broken Nature's social union,
An' justifies that ill opinion,
10   Which makes thee startle,
At me, thy poor, earth-born companion,
      An' *fellow-mortal*!

I doubt na, whyles, but thou may *thieve*;
What then? poor beastie, thou maun live!
A *daimen-icker* in a *thrave*   occasional ear, 24 sheaves
      'S a sma' request:
I'll get a blessin wi' the lave,   what's left/the rest
      An' never miss't!

Thy wee-bit *housie*, too, in ruin!
20 Its silly wa's the win's are strewin!   frail, winds
An' naething, now, to big a new ane,   build
      O' foggage green!   rank grass
An' bleak *December's winds* ensuin,
      Baith snell an' keen!   bitter

Thou saw the fields laid bare an' wast,   waste
An' weary *Winter* comin fast,
An' cozie here, beneath the blast,
      Thou thought to dwell,
Till crash! the cruel *coulter* past   iron cutter of plough
30   Out thro' thy cell.

That wee-bit heap o' leaves an' stibble,   stubble
Has cost thee monie a weary nibble!
Now thou's turn'd out, for a' thy trouble,
      But house or hald,   without refuge
To thole the Winter's *sleety dribble*,   endure
      An' *cranreuch* cauld!   hoar-frost

But Mousie, thou art no thy-lane,   not alone
In proving *foresight* may be vain:
The best laid schemes *o' Mice* an' *Men*,
40   Gang aft agley,   awry
An' lea'e us nought but grief an' pain,
      For promis'd joy!

Still, thou art blest, compar'd wi' *me*!
The *present* only toucheth thee:
But Och! I *backward* cast my e'e,   eye
      On prospects drear!
An' *forward*, tho' I canna *see*,
      I *guess* an' *fear*!

EPISTLE TO DAVIE,
A BROTHER POET

January ——

I

WHILE winds frae off BEN-LOMOND blaw,   blow
And bar the doors wi' driving snaw,   snow
   And hing us owre the ingle,   make us hang,
                     fireside
I set me down, to pass the time,
And spin a verse or twa o' rhyme,
   In hamely, *westlin* jingle.   westland
While frosty winds blaw in the drift,   fallen snow
   Ben to the chimla lug,   in, chimney corner
I grudge a wee the *Great-folk's* gift,
10   That live sae bien and snug: comfortable

I tent less, and want less   heed
    Their roomy fire-side;
But hanker, and canker,   become peevish
    To see their cursed pride.

II

It's hardly in a body's pow'r,   person's
To keep, at times, frae being sour,
    To see how things are shar'd;
How *best o' chiels* are whyles in want,   fellows
While *Coofs* on countless thousands rant,   fools, roister
20   And ken na how to wair't: spend
But DAVIE lad, ne'er fash your head,   trouble
    Tho' we hae little gear,   money
We're fit to win our daily bread,
    As lang's we're hale and fier: healthy, sound
      'Mair spier na, nor fear na,'*   ask
        Auld age ne'er mind a feg;   fig
      The last o't, the warst o't,   worst
        Is only but to beg.

III

To lye in kilns and barns at e'en,
30   When banes are craz'd, and bluid is thin,   bones
    Is, doubtless, great distress!
Yet then *content* could make us blest;
Ev'n then, sometimes we'd snatch a taste
    Of truest happiness.
The honest heart that's free frae a'
    Intended fraud or guile,
However Fortune kick the ba',   ball
    Has ay some cause to smile: always
      And mind still, you'll find still,   remember
40   A comfort this nae sma';
      Nae mair then, we'll care then,
        Nae *farther* we can *fa'*.

* Ramsay.

IV

What tho', like Commoners of air,
We wander out, we know not where,
   But either house or hal'?   *without, refuge*
Yet *Nature's* charms, the hills and woods,
The sweeping vales, and foaming floods,
   Are free alike to all.
In days when Daisies deck the ground,
50   And Blackbirds whistle clear,
With honest joy, our hearts will bound,
   To see the *coming* year:
    On braes when we please then,   *hill-sides*
       We'll sit and *sowth* a tune;   *'try over with a low whistle' (B)*
    Syne *rhyme* till't, we'll time till't   *then, to it*
       And sing't when we hae done.

V

It's no in titles nor in rank;
It's no in wealth like *Lon'on Bank*,
   To purchase peace and rest;
60 It's no in makin muckle, *mair*:
It's no in books; it's no in Lear,   *learning*
   To make us truly blest:
If Happiness hae not her seat
   And center in the breast,
We may be *wise*, or *rich*, or *great*,
   But never can be *blest*:
    Nae treasures, nor pleasures
       Could make us happy lang;   *for long*
    The *heart* ay's the part ay,
70   That makes us right or wrang.   *wrong*

VI

Think ye, that sic as *you* and *I*,
Wha drudge and drive thro' wet and dry,
   Wi' never-ceasing toil;
Think ye, are we less blest than they,
Wha scarcely tent us in their way,

As hardly worth their while?
Alas! how aft, in haughty mood,
   GOD'S creatures they oppress!
Or else, neglecting a' that's guid,
80   They riot in excess!
        Baith careless, and fearless,
           Of either Heaven or Hell;
        Esteeming, and deeming,
           It a' an idle tale!

VII

Then let us chearfu' acquiesce;
Nor make our scanty Pleasures less,
   By pining at our state:
And, ev'n should Misfortunes come,
I, here whae sit, hae met wi' some,
90   An's thankfu' for them yet.   *and am*
They gie the wit of *Age* to *Youth*;
   They let us ken oursel;
They make us see the naked truth,
   The *real* guid and ill.
      Tho' losses, and crosses,
         Be lessons right severe,
      There's *wit* there, ye'll get there,
         Ye'll find nae other where.

VIII

But tent me, DAVIE, *Ace o' Hearts*!
100 (To say aught less wad wrang the *cartes*,   *cards*
   And flatt'ry I detest)
This life has joys for you and I;
And joys that riches ne'er could buy;
   And joys the very best.
There's a' the *Pleasures o' the Heart*,
   The *Lover* and the *Frien'*;
Ye hae your MEG, your dearest part,
   And I my darling JEAN!

It warms me, it charms me,
110   To mention but her *name*:
It heats me, it beets me,   kindles
        And sets me a' on flame!

IX

O, all ye *Pow'rs* who rule above!
O THOU, whose very self art *love*!
    THOU know'st my words sincere!
The *life blood* streaming thro' my heart,
Or my more dear *Immortal part*,
    Is not more fondly dear!
When heart-corroding care and grief
120   Deprive my soul of rest,
Her dear idea brings relief,
    And solace to my breast.
        Thou BEING, Allseeing,
                O hear my fervent pray'r!
        Still take her, and make her,
                THY most peculiar care!

X

All hail! ye tender feelings dear!
The smile of love, the friendly tear,
    The sympathetic glow!
130 Long since, this world's thorny ways
Had number'd out my weary days,
    Had it not been for you!
Fate still has blest me with a friend,
    In ev'ry care and ill;
And oft a more *endearing* band,
    A *tye* more tender still.
        It lightens, it brightens,
                The tenebrific scene,   dark, gloomy
        To meet with, and greet with,
140   My DAVIE or my JEAN!

XI

O, how that *name* inspires my style!
The words come skelpan, rank and file,   spanking
   Amaist before I ken!
The ready measure rins as fine,   runs
As *Phoebus* and the famous *Nine*   as if
   Were glowran owre my pen.   gazing
My spavet *Pegasus* will limp,   spavined/halting
   Till ance he's fairly het;   hot
And then he'll hilch, and stilt, and jimp,   hobble, limp, jump
150   And rin an unco fit: uncommon pace
     But least then, the beast then,   lest
      Should rue this hasty ride,
     I'll light now, and dight now,   wipe
      His sweaty, wizen'd hide.

THE LAMENT

Occasioned by the Unfortunate Issue of
A FRIEND'S AMOUR

Alas! how oft does goodness wound itself!
And sweet Affection *prove the spring of Woe!*

                      Home

I

O Thou pale Orb, that silent shines,
   While care-untroubled mortals sleep!
Thou seest a *wretch*, who inly pines,
   And wanders here to wail and weep!
With Woe I nightly vigils keep,
   Beneath thy wan, unwarming beam;
And mourn, in lamentation deep,
   How *life* and *love* are all a dream!

II

I joyless view thy rays adorn,
10   The faintly-marked, distant hill:
I joyless view thy trembling horn,
    Reflected in the gurgling rill.
My fondly-fluttering heart, be still!
    Thou busy pow'r, Remembrance, cease!
Ah! must the agonizing thrill,
    For ever bar returning Peace!

III

No idly-feign'd, poetic pains,
    My sad, lovelorn lamentings claim:
No shepherd's pipe – Arcadian strains;
20   No fabled tortures, quaint and tame.
The *plighted faith*; the *mutual flame*;
    The *oft-attested Powers above*;
The promis'd Father's tender name;
    These were the pledges of my love!

IV

Encircled in her clasping arms,
    How have the raptur'd moments flown!
How have I wish'd for Fortune's charms,
    For her dear sake, and her's alone!
And, must I think it! is she gone,
30   My secret-heart's exulting boast?
And does she heedless hear my groan?
    And is she ever, ever lost?

V

Oh! can she bear so base a heart,
    So lost to Honor, lost to Truth,
As from the *fondest lover* part,
    The *plighted husband* of her youth?
Alas! Life's path may be unsmooth!
    Her way may lie thro' rough distress!
Then, who her pangs and pains will soothe,
40   Her sorrows share and make them less?

VI

Ye winged Hours that o'er us past,
   Enraptur'd more, the more enjoy'd,
Your dear remembrance in my breast,
   My fondly-treasur'd thoughts employ'd.
That breast, how dreary now, and void,
   For her too scanty once of room!
Ev'n ev'ry *ray* of *Hope* destroy'd,
   And not a *Wish* to gild the gloom!

VII

The morn that warns th'approaching day,
50   Awakes me up to toil and woe:
I see the hours, in long array,
   That I must suffer, lingering, slow.
Full many a pang, and many a throe,
   Keen Recollection's direful train,
Must wring my soul, ere Phoebus, low,
   Shall kiss the distant, western main.

VIII

And when my nightly couch I try,
   Sore-harass'd out, with care and grief,
My toil-beat nerves, and tear-worn eye,
60   Keep watchings with the nightly thief:
Or if I slumber, Fancy, chief,
   Reigns, haggard-wild, in sore afright:
Ev'n day, all-bitter, brings relief,
   From such a horror-breathing night.

IX

O! thou bright Queen, who, o'er th'expanse,
   Now highest reign'st, with boundless sway!
Oft has thy silent-marking glance
   Observ'd us, fondly-wand'ring, stray!
The time, unheeded, sped away,
70   While Love's *luxurious pulse* beat high,
Beneath thy silver-gleaming ray,
   To mark the mutual-kindling eye.

X

Oh! scenes in strong remembrance set!
  Scenes, never, never to return!
Scenes, if in stupor I forget,
  Again I feel, again I burn!
From ev'ry joy and pleasure torn,
  Life's weary vale I'll wander thro';
And hopeless, comfortless, I'll mourn
80   *A faithless woman's broken vow.*

DESPONDENCY,
AN ODE

I

OPPRESS'D with grief, oppress'd with care,
A burden more than I can bear,
  I set me down and sigh:
O Life! Thou art a galling load,
Along a rough, a weary road,
  To wretches such as I!
Dim-backward as I cast my view,
  What sick'ning Scenes appear!
What Sorrows *yet* may pierce me thro',
10   Too justly I may fear!
      Still caring, despairing,
        Must be my bitter doom;
      My woes here, shall close ne'er,
        But with the *closing tomb*!

II

Happy! ye sons of Busy-life,
Who, equal to the bustling strife,
  No other view regard!
Ev'n when the wished *end's* deny'd,
Yet while the busy *means* are ply'd,
20   They bring their own reward:
Whilst I, a hope-abandon'd wight,

Unfitted with an *aim*,
Meet ev'ry sad-returning night,
   And joyless morn the same.
     You, bustling and justling,
       Forget each grief and pain;
    I, listless, yet restless,
       Find ev'ry prospect vain.

III

How blest the Solitary's lot,
Who, all-forgetting, all-forgot,
   Within his humble cell,
The cavern wild with tangling roots,
Sits o'er his newly-gather'd fruits,
   Beside his crystal well!
Or haply, to his ev'ning thought,
   By unfrequented stream,
The *ways of men* are distant brought,
   A faint-collected dream:
     While praising, and raising
       His thoughts to Heaven on high,
    As wand'ring, meand'ring,
       He views the solemn sky.

IV

Than I, no *lonely Hermit* plac'd
Where never human footstep trac'd,
   Less fit to play the part,
The *lucky moment* to improve,
And *just* to stop, and *just* to move,
   With *self-respecting* art:
But ah! those pleasures, Loves and Joys,
   Which I too keenly taste,
The *Solitary* can despise,
   Can want, and yet be blest!
     He needs not, he heeds not,
       Or human love or hate;
    Whilst I here, must cry here,
       At perfidy ingrate!

V

Oh, enviable, early days,
When dancing thoughtless Pleasure's maze,
   To Care, to Guilt unknown!
60 How ill exchang'd for riper times,
To feel the follies, or the crimes,
   Of others, or my own!
Ye tiny elves that guiltless sport,
   Like linnets in the bush,
Ye little know the ills ye court,
   When Manhood is your wish!
     The losses, the crosses,
       That *active man* engage;
     The fears all, the tears all,
70   Of dim declining *Age*!

MAN WAS MADE TO MOURN,
A DIRGE

I

WHEN chill November's surly blast
   Made fields and forests bare,
One ev'ning, as I wand'red forth,
   Along the banks of AIRE,
I spy'd a man, whose aged step
   Seem'd weary, worn with care;
His face was furrow'd o'er with years,
   And hoary was his hair.

II

Young stranger, whither wand'rest thou?
10   Began the rev'rend Sage;
Does thirst of wealth thy step constrain,
   Or youthful Pleasure's rage?

Or haply, prest with cares and woes,
   Too soon thou hast began,
To wander forth, with me, to mourn
   The miseries of Man.

III

The Sun that overhangs yon moors,
   Out-spreading far and wide,
Where hundreds labour to support
20   A haughty lordling's pride;
I've seen yon weary winter-sun
   Twice forty times return;
And ev'ry time has added proofs,
   That Man was made to mourn.

IV

O Man! while in thy early years,
   How prodigal of time!
Misspending all thy precious hours,
   Thy glorious, youthful prime!
Alternate Follies take the sway;
30   Licentious Passions burn;
Which tenfold force gives Nature's law,
   That Man was made to mourn.

V

Look not alone on youthful Prime,
   Or Manhood's active might;
Man then is useful to his kind,
   Supported is his right:
But see him on the edge of life,
   With Cares and Sorrows worn,
Then Age and Want, Oh! ill-match'd pair!
40   Show Man was made to mourn.

VI

A few seem favourites of Fate,
   In Pleasure's lap carest;
Yet, think not all the Rich and Great,
   Are likewise truly blest.
But Oh! what crouds in ev'ry land,
   All wretched and forlorn,
Thro' weary life this lesson learn,
   That Man was made to mourn!

VII

Many and sharp the num'rous Ills
50   Inwoven with our frame!
More pointed still we make ourselves,
   Regret, Remorse and Shame!
And Man, whose heav'n-erected face,
   The smiles of love adorn,
Man's inhumanity to Man
   Makes countless thousands mourn!

VIII

See, yonder poor, o'erlabour'd wight,
   So abject, mean and vile,
Who begs a brother of the earth
60   To give him leave to toil;
And see his lordly *fellow-worm*,
   The poor petition spurn,
Unmindful, tho' a weeping wife,
   And helpless offspring mourn.

IX

If I'm design'd yon lordling's slave,
   By Nature's law design'd,
Why was an independent wish
   E'er planted in my mind?
If not, why am I subject to
70   His cruelty, or scorn?
Or why has Man the will and pow'r
   To make his fellow mourn?

X

Yet, let not this too much, my Son,
    Disturb thy youthful breast:
This partial view of human-kind
    Is surely not the *last*!
The poor, oppressed, honest man
    Had never, sure, been born,
Had there not been some recompence
80   To comfort those that mourn!

XI

O Death! the poor man's dearest friend,
    The kindest and the best!
Welcome the hour, my aged limbs
    Are laid with thee at rest!
The Great, the Wealthy fear thy blow,
    From pomp and pleasure torn;
But Oh! a blest relief for those
    That weary-laden mourn!

WINTER,
A DIRGE

I

THE Wintry West extends his blast,
    And hail and rain does blaw;   blow
Or, the stormy North sends driving forth,
    The blinding sleet and snaw: snow
While, tumbling brown, the Burn comes down,
    And roars frae bank to brae;   hillside
And bird and beast, in covert, rest,
    And pass the heartless day.

II

'The sweeping blast, the sky o'ercast,'*
10   The joyless *winter-day*,
Let others fear, to me more dear,
        Than all the pride of May:
The Tempest's howl, it *soothes* my soul,
        My *griefs* it seems to join;
The leafless trees my fancy please,
        Their *fate* resembles mine!

III

Thou POW'R SUPREME, whose mighty Scheme,
        These *woes* of mine fulfil;
Here, firm, I rest, they *must* be best,
20   Because they are *Thy* Will!
Then all I want (Oh, do thou grant
        This one request of mine!)
Since to *enjoy* Thou dost deny,
        Assist me to *resign*!

A PRAYER,
IN THE PROSPECT OF DEATH

I

O THOU unknown, Almighty Cause
        Of all my hope and fear!
In whose dread Presence, ere an hour,
        Perhaps I must appear!

II

If I have wander'd in those paths
        Of life I ought to shun;
As *Something*, loudly, in my breast,
        Remonstrates I have done;

* Dr. Young

III

Thou know'st that Thou hast formed me,
10   With Passions wild and strong;
And list'ning to their witching voice
    Has often led me wrong.

IV

Where human *weakness* has come short,
    Or *frailty* stept aside,
Do Thou, ALL-GOOD, for such Thou art,
    In shades of darkness hide.

V

Where with *intention* I have err'd,
    No other plea I have,
But, *Thou art good*; and Goodness still
20   Delighteth to forgive.

TO A MOUNTAIN-DAISY,

*On turning one down, with the Plough,
in April —— 1786*

WEE, modest, crimson-tipped flow'r,
Thou's met me in an evil hour;
For I maun crush amang the stoure   dust
        Thy slender stem:
To spare thee now is past my pow'r,
        Thou bonie gem.

Alas! it's no thy neebor sweet,   neighbour
The bonie *Lark*, companion meet!
Bending thee 'mang the dewy weet!   wet
10   Wi's spreckl'd breast,
When upward-springing, blythe, to greet
        The purpling East.

Cauld blew the bitter-biting *North*
Upon thy early, humble birth;
Yet chearfully thou glinted forth
     Amid the storm,
Scarce rear'd above the *Parent-earth*
      Thy tender form.

The flaunting *flow'rs* our Gardens yield,
20 High-shelt'ring woods and wa's maun shield,
But thou, beneath the random bield   shelter
     O' clod or stane,   stone
Adorns the histie *stibble-field*,   bare, stubble-
      Unseen, alane.   alone

There, in thy scanty mantle clad,
Thy snawie bosom sun-ward spread,   snowy
Thou lifts thy unassuming head
     In humble guise;
But now the *share* uptears thy bed,   ploughshare
30   And low thou lies!

Such is the fate of artless Maid,
Sweet *flow'ret* of the rural shade!
By Love's simplicity betray'd,
     And guileless trust,
Till she, like thee, all soil'd, is laid
      Low i' the dust.

Such is the fate of simple Bard,
On Life's rough ocean luckless starr'd!
Unskilful he to note the card
40   Of *prudent Lore*,
Till billows rage, and gales blow hard,
      And whelm him o'er!

Such fate to *suffering worth* is giv'n,
Who long with wants and woes has striv'n,
By human pride or cunning driv'n

To Mis'ry's brink,
Till wrench'd of ev'ry stay but HEAV'N,
He, ruin'd, sink!

Ev'n thou who mourn'st the *Daisy's* fate,
That fate is thine – no distant date;
Stern Ruin's *plough-share* drives, elate,
Full on thy bloom,
Till crush'd beneath the *furrow's* weight,
Shall be thy doom!

TO RUIN

I

ALL hail! inexorable lord!
At whose destruction-breathing word,
The mightiest empires fall!
Thy cruel, woe-delighted train,
The ministers of Grief and Pain,
A sullen welcome, all!
With stern-resolv'd, despairing eye,
I see each aimed dart;
For one has cut my *dearest tye*,
And quivers in my heart.
Then low'ring, and pouring,
The *Storm* no more I dread;
Tho' thick'ning, and black'ning,
Round my devoted head.

II

And thou grim Pow'r, by Life abhorr'd,
While Life a *pleasure* can afford,
Oh! hear a wretch's pray'r!
No more I shrink appall'd, afraid;
I court, I beg thy friendly aid,
To close this scene of care!

When shall my soul, in silent peace,
  Resign Life's *joyless* day?
My weary heart its throbbings cease,
  Cold-mould'ring in the clay?
    No fear more, no tear more,
      To stain my lifeless face,
    Enclasped, and grasped,
      Within thy cold embrace!

EPISTLE
TO A YOUNG FRIEND
May —— 1786

I

I Lang hae thought, my youthfu' friend,
  A Something to have sent you,
Tho' it should serve nae other end
  Than just a kind memento;
But how the subject theme may gang,
  Let time and chance determine;
Perhaps it may turn out a Sang;
  Perhaps, turn out a Sermon.

II

Ye'll try the world soon my lad,
10   And ANDREW dear believe me,
Ye'll find mankind an unco squad,
  And muckle they may grieve ye:
For care and trouble set your thought,
  Ev'n when your end's attained;
And a' your views may come to nought,
  Where ev'ry nerve is strained.

III

I'll no say, men are villains a';
   The real, harden'd wicked,
Whae hae nae check but *human law*,
20   Are to a few restricked:
But Och, mankind are unco weak,
   An' little to be trusted;
If *Self* the wavering balance shake,
   It's rarely right adjusted!

IV

Yet they wha fa' in Fortune's strife,
   Their fate we should na censure,
For still th'*important end* of life,
   They equally may answer:
A man may hae an *honest heart*,
30   Tho' Poortith hourly stare him;   poverty
A man may tak a neebor's part,   neighbour's
   Yet hae nae *cash* to spare him.

V

Ay free, aff han', your story tell,   offhand
   When wi' a bosom crony;
But still keep something to yoursel
   Ye scarcely tell to ony.
Conceal yoursel as weel's ye can
   Frae critical dissection;
But keek thro' ev'ry other man,   look/pry
40   Wi' sharpen'd, sly inspection.

VI

The *sacred lowe* o' weel plac'd love,   flame
   Luxuriantly indulge it;
But never tempt th'*illicit rove*,   attempt
   Tho' naething should divulge it:
I waive the quantum o' the sin;   amount
   The hazard of concealing;
But Och! it hardens *a' within*,
   And petrifies the feeling!

VII

To catch Dame Fortune's golden smile,
50   Assiduous wait upon her;
And gather gear by ev'ry wile,   money/property
    That's justify'd by Honor:
Not for to *hide* it in a *hedge*,
    Nor for a *train-attendant*;
But for the glorious priviledge
    Of being *independant*.

VIII

The fear o' Hell's a hangman's whip,
    To haud the wretch in order;   hold
But where ye feel your *Honor* grip,
60   Let that ay be your border:
Its slightest touches, instant pause –
    Debar a' side-pretences;
And resolutely keep its laws,
    Uncaring consequences.

IX

The great CREATOR to revere,
    Must sure become the *Creature*;
But still the preaching cant forbear,
    And ev'n the rigid feature:
Yet ne'er with Wits prophane to range,
70   Be complaisance extended;
An *atheist-laugh's* a poor exchange
    For *Deity offended*!

X

When ranting round in Pleasure's ring,   frolicking
    Religion may be blinded;
Or if she gie a *random-fling*,
    It may be little minded;
But when on Life we're tempest-driven,
    A Conscience but a canker –
A correspondence fix'd wi' Heav'n,
80   Is sure a noble *anchor*!

XI

Adieu, dear, amiable Youth!
   Your *heart* can ne'er be wanting!
May Prudence, Fortitude and Truth
   Erect your brow undaunting!
In *ploughman phrase* 'GOD send you speed,'
   Still daily to grow wiser;
And may ye better reck the *rede*,   heed the advice
   Than ever did th' *Adviser*!

ON A SCOTCH BARD
GONE TO THE WEST INDIES

A' ye wha live by sowps o' drink,   mouthfuls
A' ye wha live by crambo-clink,   rhyme
A' ye wha live and never think,
      Come, mourn wi' me!
Our *billie's* gien us a' a jink,   comrade, slip
      An' owre the Sea.

Lament him a' ye rantan core,   merry company
Wha dearly like a random-splore;   frolic
Nae mair he'll join the *merry roar*,
10   In social key;
For now he's taen anither shore,
      An' owre the Sea!

The bonie lasses weel may wiss him,   wish
And in their dear *petitions* place him:
The widows, wives, an' a' may bless him,
      Wi' tearfu' e'e;   eye
For weel I wat they'll sairly miss him   know
      That's owre the Sea!

O Fortune, they hae room to grumble!
Hadst thou taen aff some drowsy bummle,   bungler
Wha can do nought but fyke an' fumble,   fuss
     'Twad been nae plea;
But he was gleg as onie wumble,   nimble, gimlet
     That's owre the Sea!

Auld, cantie KYLE may weepers wear,   cheerful
An' stain them wi' the saut, saut tear: salt
'Twill mak her poor, auld heart, I fear,
     In flinders flee: fragments
He was her *Laureat* monie a year,
     That's owre the Sea!

He saw Misfortune's cauld *Nor-west*
Lang-mustering up a bitter blast;
A Jillet brak his heart at last,   jilt
     Ill may she be!
So, took a birth afore the mast,   berth
     An' owre the Sea.

To tremble under Fortune's cummock;   cudgel
On scarce a bellyfu' o' *drummock*,   meal and water
Wi' his proud, independant stomach,
     Could ill agree;
So, row't his hurdies in a *hammock*,   rolled, buttocks
     An' owre the Sea.

He ne'er was gien to great misguidin,
Yet coin his pouches wad na bide in;   pockets
Wi' him it ne'er was *under hidin*;
     He dealt it free:
The *Muse* was a' that he took pride in,
     That's owre the Sea.

Jamaica bodies, use him weel,
An' hap him in a cozie biel: wrap, shelter
Ye'll find him ay a dainty chiel,   pleasant fellow

An' fou o' glee: full
He wad na wrang'd the vera *Diel*,   wronged, very,
                            Devil
    That's owre the Sea.

Fareweel, my *rhyme-composing billie*!   fellow
Your native soil was right ill-willie;   unkind
But may ye flourish like a lily,
    Now bonilie!
I'll toast you in my hindmost *gillie*,   last gill
60   Tho' owre the Sea!

A DEDICATION
TO G**** H******* Esq;

EXPECT na, Sir, in this narration,
A fleechan, fleth'ran *Dedication*,   flattering,
                          wheedling
To roose you up, an' ca' you guid,   praise
An' sprung o' great an' noble bluid;
Because ye're sirnam'd like *His Grace*,
Perhaps related to the race:
Then when I'm tir'd – and sae are *ye*,
Wi' monie a fulsome, sinfu' lie,
Set up a face, how I stop short,
10 For fear your modesty be hurt.

    This may do – maun do, Sir, wi' them wha
Maun please the Great-folk for a wamefou; bellyful
For me! sae laigh I need na bow,   low
For, LORD be thanket, *I can plough*;
And when I downa yoke a naig,   cannot, small horse
Then, LORD be thanket, *I can beg*;
Sae I shall say, an' that's nae flatt'rin,
It's just *sic Poet* an' *sic Patron*.

The Poet, some guid Angel help him,
20 Or else, I fear, some *ill ane* skelp him!   slap
He may do weel for a' he's done yet,
But only – he's no just begun yet.

The Patron, (Sir, ye maun forgie me,   forgive
I winna lie, come what will o' me)   will not
On ev'ry hand it will allow'd be,
He's just – nae better than he should be.

I readily and freely grant,
He downa see a poor man want;
What's no his ain, he winna tak it;   own
30 What ance he says, he winna break it;
Ought he can lend he'll no refus't,   anything
Till aft his guidness is abus'd;
And rascals whyles that do him wrang,   wrong
Ev'n *that*, he does na mind it lang: remember
As Master, Landlord, Husband, Father,
He does na fail his part in either.

But then, nae thanks to him for a' that;
Nae *godly symptom* ye can ca' that;
It's naething but a milder feature,
40 Of our poor, sinfu', corrupt Nature:
Ye'll get the best o' moral works,
'Mang black *Gentoos*, and Pagan *Turks*,
Or Hunters wild on *Ponotaxi*,
Wha never heard of Orth-d-xy.
That he's the poor man's friend in need,
The GENTLEMAN in word and deed,
It's no through terror of D-mn-t-n;
It's just a carnal inclination,
And Och! that's nae r-g-n-r-t-n!

50 Morality, thou deadly bane,
Thy tens o' thousands thou hast slain!
Vain is his hope, whase stay an' trust is,
In *moral* Mercy, Truth and Justice!

No – stretch a point to catch a plack;   farthing
Abuse a Brother to his back;
Steal thro' the *winnock* frae a wh-re,   window
But point the Rake that taks the *door*;
Be to the Poor like onie whunstane,   whinstone
And haud their noses to the grunstane;   hold, grindstone
60 Ply ev'ry art o' *legal* thieving;
No matter – stick to *sound believing*.

Learn three-mile pray'rs, an' half-mile graces,
Wi' weel spread looves, an' lang, wry faces;   palms
Grunt up a solemn, lengthen'd groan,
And damn a' Parties but your own;
I'll warrant then, ye're nae Deceiver,
A steady, sturdy, staunch *Believer*.

O ye wha leave the springs o' C-lv-n,
For *gumlie dubs* of your ain delvin!   muddy puddles, digging
70 Ye sons of Heresy and Error,
Ye'll *some day* squeel in quaking terror!
When Vengeance draws the sword in wrath,
And in the fire throws the *sheath*;
When Ruin, with his sweeping *besom*,
Just frets till Heav'n commission gies him;
While o'er the *Harp* pale Misery moans,
And strikes the ever-deep'ning tones,
Still louder shrieks, and heavier groans!

Your pardon, Sir, for this digression,
80 I maist forgat my *Dedication*;
But when Divinity comes cross me,
My readers then are sure to lose me.

So Sir, you see 'twas nae daft vapour,   whimsy
But I maturely thought it proper,
When a' my works I did review,
To *dedicate* them, Sir, to YOU:
Because (ye need na tak it ill)
I thought them something like *yoursel*.

Then patronize them wi' your favor,
90   And your Petitioner shall ever –
I had amaist said, *ever pray*,
But that's a word I need na say:
For prayin I hae little skill o't;
I'm baith dead-sweer, an' wretched ill o't;   very reluctant, poor at it
But I'se repeat each poor man's *pray'r*,   I'll
That kens or hears about you, Sir –
'May ne'er Misfortune's gowling bark,   yelling
Howl thro' the dwelling o' the CLERK!
May ne'er his gen'rous, honest heart,
100   For that same gen'rous spirit smart!
May K******'s far-honor'd name   [Kennedy's]
Lang beet his hymeneal flame,   feed
Till H*******'s, at least a diz'n,   [Hamilton's] dozen
Are frae their nuptial labors risen:
Five bonie Lasses round their table,
And sev'n braw fellows, stout an' able,
To serve their King an' Country weel,
By word, or pen, or pointed steel!
May Health and Peace, with mutual rays,
110   Shine on the ev'ning o' his days;
Till his wee, curlie *John's* ier-oe,   great-grandchild
When ebbing life nae mair shall flow,
The last, sad, mournful rites bestow!'

I will not wind a lang conclusion,
With complimentary effusion:
But whilst your wishes and endeavours,
Are blest with Fortune's smiles and favours,
I am, Dear Sir, with zeal most fervent,
Your much indebted, humble servant.

120   But if, which Pow'rs above prevent,
That iron-hearted Carl, *Want*,   fellow
Attended, in his grim advances,
By *sad mistakes*, and *black mischances*,

While hopes, and joys, and pleasures fly him,
Make you as poor a dog as I am,
Your *humble servant* then no more;
For who would humbly serve the Poor?
But by a poor man's hopes in Heav'n!
While recollection's pow'r is giv'n,
130   If, in the vale of humble life,
The victim sad of Fortune's strife,
I, through the tender-gushing tear,
Should recognise my *Master dear*,
If friendless, low, we meet together,
Then, Sir, your hand – my FRIEND and BROTHER.

TO A LOUSE,

On Seeing one on a Lady's Bonnet at Church

HA! whare ye gaun, ye crowlan ferlie!   crawling wonder
Your impudence protects you sairly: indeed
I canna say but ye strunt rarely,   strut
    Owre *gawze* and *lace*;
Tho' faith, I fear ye dine but sparely,
    On sic a place.

Ye ugly, creepan, blastet wonner,   wonder
Detested, shunn'd, by saunt an' sinner,   saint
How daur ye set your fit upon her,   dare, foot
10   Sae fine a *Lady*!
Gae somewhere else and seek your dinner,
    On some poor body.

Swith, in some beggar's haffet squattle;   off!, temple, squat
There ye may creep, and sprawl, and sprattle,   scramble
Wi' ither kindred, jumping cattle,   beasts
    In shoals and nations;   families, tribes
Whare *horn* nor *bane* ne'er daur unsettle,   horn, bone
    Your thick plantations.

Now haud you there, ye're out of sight,　　keep
20　Below the fatt'rels, snug and tight,　　falderals
Na faith ye yet! ye'll no be right,
　　　Till ye've got on it,
The vera tapmost, towrin height　　very topmost
　　　O' *Miss's bonnet*.

My sooth! right bauld ye set your nose out,　　bold
As plump an' gray as onie grozet:　　gooseberry
O for some rank, mercurial rozet,　　resin
　　　Or fell, red smeddum,　　deadly, powder
I'd gie you sic a hearty dose o't,
30　　　Wad dress your droddum!　　thrash, backside

I wad na been surpriz'd to spy
You on an auld wife's *flainen toy*;　　flannel cap
Or aiblins some bit duddie boy,　　perhaps, small ragged
　　　On's *wylecoat*;　　flannel vest
But Miss's fine *Lunardi*, fye!　　balloon bonnet
　　　How daur ye do't?

O *Jenny* dinna toss your head,　　do not
An' set your beauties a' abroad!　　abroad
Ye little ken what cursed speed
40　　　The blastie's makin!　　ill-disposed creature
Thae *winks* and *finger-ends*, I dread,　　those
　　　Are notice takin!

O wad some Pow'r the giftie gie us　　little gift
To see oursels as others see us!
It wad frae monie a blunder free us
　　　An' foolish notion:
What airs in dress an' gait wad lea'e us
　　　And ev'n Devotion!

EPISTLE TO J. L*****K,
AN OLD SCOTCH BARD

April 1st, 1785

WHILE briers an' woodbines budding green,
An' Paitricks scraichan loud at e'en,   *partridges, screaming, evening*
And morning Poossie whiddan seen,   *hare, scudding*
      Inspire my Muse,
This freedom, in an *unknown* frien',
      I pray excuse.

On Fasteneen we had a rockin,   *Shrove Tuesday, spinning party*
To ca' the crack and weave our stockin;   *have a chat*
And there was muckle fun and jokin,
10   Ye need na doubt;
At length we had a hearty yokin,   *set-to*
      At *sang about*.   *singing in turn*

There was ae *sang*, amang the rest,
Aboon them a' it pleas'd me best,   *above*
That some kind husband had addrest,
      To some sweet wife:
It thirl'd the heart-strings thro' the breast, *thrilled*
      A' to the life.

I've scarce heard ought describ'd sae weel,
20 What gen'rous, manly bosoms feel;
Thought I, 'Can this be *Pope*, or *Steele*,
      Or *Beattie's* wark;'   *work*
They told me 'twas an odd kind chiel   *told, fellow*
      About *Muirkirk*.

It pat me fidgean-fain to hear't,   *put, tingling with pleasure*
An' sae about him there I spier't;   *asked*
Then a' that kent him round declar'd,
      He had *ingine*,   *wit*
That nane excell'd it, few cam near't,
30   It was sae fine.

That set him to a pint of ale,
An' either douse or merry tale,   sober
Or rhymes an' sangs he'd made himsel,
  Or witty catches,
'Tween Inverness and Teviotdale,
  He had few matches.

Then up I gat, an swoor an aith,   swore, oath
Tho' I should pawn my pleugh an' graith,   plough, harness
Or die a cadger pownie's death,   hawker pony's
40 At some dyke-back,   behind a wall
A *pint* an' *gill* I'd gie them *baith*,
  To hear your crack.   talk

But first an' foremost, I should tell,
Amaist as soon as I could spell,
I to the *crambo-jingle* fell,   rhyming
  Tho' rude an' rough,
Yet crooning to a body's sel,   humming, to
        oneself
  Does weel eneugh.   enough

I am nae *Poet*, in a sense,
50 But just a *Rhymer* like by chance,
An' hae to Learning nae pretence,
  Yet, what the matter?
Whene'er my Muse does on me glance,
  I jingle at her.

Your Critic-folk may cock their nose,
And say, 'How can you e'er propose,
You wha ken hardly *verse* frae *prose*,
  To mak a *sang*?'
But by your leaves, my learned foes,
60 Ye're maybe wrang.   wrong

What's a' your jargon o' your Schools,
Your Latin names for horns an' stools;
If honest Nature made you *fools*,

> What sairs your Grammars?   serves
> Ye'd better taen up *spades* and *shools*,   shovels
> Or *knappin-hammers*.   stone-breaking

> A set o' dull, conceited Hashes,   dunderheads
> Confuse their brains in *Colledge-classes*!
> They *gang in* Stirks, and *come out* Asses,   steers/young bullocks
> 70   Plain truth to speak;
> An' syne they think to climb Parnassus   then
> By dint o' Greek!

> Gie me ae spark o' Nature's fire,
> That's a' the learning I desire;
> Then tho' I drudge thro' dub an' mire   puddle
> At pleugh or cart,
> My Muse, tho' hamely in attire,
> May touch the heart.

> O for a spunk o' ALLAN'S glee,   spark
> 80 Or FERGUSON'S, the bauld an' slee,   bold, clever
> Or bright L*****K'S, my friend to be,
> If I can hit it!
> That would be *lear* eneugh for me,   learning
> If I could get it.

> Now, Sir, if ye hae friends enow,   enough
> Tho' *real friends* I b'lieve are few,
> Yet, if your catalogue be fow,   full
> I'se no insist;   I'll
> But gif ye want ae friend that's true,   if
> 90   I'm on your list.

> I winna blaw about *mysel*,   will not brag
> As ill I like my fauts to tell;   faults
> But friends an' folk that wish me well,
> They sometimes roose me;   praise
> Tho' I maun own, as monie still,
> As far abuse me.

There's ae *wee faut* they whiles lay to me,
I like the lasses – Gude forgie me!   God forgive
For monie a Plack they wheedle frae me,   coin
100   At dance or fair:
Maybe some *ither thing* they gie me
          They weel can spare.

But MAUCHLINE Race or MAUCHLINE Fair,
I should be proud to meet you there;
We'se gie ae night's discharge to *care*,   we'll
          If we forgather,
An' hae a swap o' *rhymin-ware*,
          Wi' ane anither.

The *four-gill chap*, we'se gar him clatter,   cup, we'll make
110 An' kirs'n him wi' reekin water;   christen, steaming
Syne we'll sit down an' tak our whitter,   draught
          To chear our heart;
An' faith, we'se be *acquainted* better
          Before we part.

Awa ye selfish, warly race,   worldly
Wha think that havins, sense an' grace,   manners
Ev'n love an' friendship should give place
          To *catch-the-plack*!   coining money
I dinna like to see your face,   do not
120   Nor hear your crack.

But ye whom social pleasure charms,
Whose hearts the *tide of kindness* warms,
Who hold your *being* on the terms,
          'Each aids the others,'
Come to my bowl, come to my arms,
          My friends, my brothers!

But to conclude my lang epistle,
As my auld pen's worn to the grissle;
Twa lines frae you wad gar me fissle,   make, tingle
130   Who am, most fervent,
While I can either sing, or whissle,
          Your friend and servant.

TO THE SAME

April 21st, 1785

WHILE new-ca'd kye rowte at the stake,
An' pownies reek in pleugh or braik,
This hour on e'enin's edge I take,
    To own I'm debtor,
To honest-hearted, auld L*****k,
        For his kind *letter*.

Forjesket sair, with weary legs,
Rattlin the corn out-owre the rigs,
Or dealing thro' amang the naigs
10   Their ten-hours bite,
My awkwart Muse sair pleads and begs,
        I would na write.

The tapetless, ramfeezl'd hizzie,
She's saft at best an' something lazy,
Quo' she, 'Ye ken we've been sae busy
        This month an' mair,
That trouth, my head is grown right dizzie,
        An' something sair.'

Her dowf excuses pat me mad;
20 'Conscience,' says I, 'ye thowless jad!
I'll write, an' that a hearty blaud,
        This vera night;
So dinna ye affront your trade,
        But rhyme it right.

'Shall bauld L*****K, the *king o' hearts*,
Tho' mankind were a *pack o' cartes*,
Roose you sae weel for your deserts,
        In terms sae friendly,
Yet ye'll neglect to shaw your parts
30   An' thank him kindly?'

Glosses (right margin):

- newly calved cattle, low
- ponies, smoke, plough, harrow
- evening's
- sorely 'jaded with fatigue' (B)
- ridges
- distributing, nags
- heedless, exhausted hussy
- silly
- weak, put
- spiritless wench
- screed
- very
- do not
- bold
- praise
- show

Sae I gat paper in a blink,   twinkling
An' down gaed *stumpie* in the ink: worn quill pen
Quoth I, 'Before I sleep a wink,
    I vow I'll close it;
An' if ye winna mak it clink,   will not, rhyme
    By Jove I'll prose it!'

Sae I've begun to scrawl, but whether
In rhyme, or prose, or baith thegither,
Or some hotch-potch that's rightly neither,
40   Let time mak proof;
But I shall scribble down some blether   nonsense
    Just clean aff-loof.   'unpremeditated' (B)

My worthy friend, ne'er grudge an' carp,
Tho' Fortune use you hard an' sharp;
Come, kittle up your *moorlan harp*   tickle
    Wi' gleesome touch!
Ne'er mind how Fortune *waft* an' *warp*;   weave
    She's but a b-tch.

She's gien me monie a jirt an' fleg,   jerk, scare
50 Sin I could striddle owre a rig;   since, straddle
But by the L—d, tho' I should beg
    Wi' lyart pow,   grey head
I'll laugh, an' sing, an' shake my leg,   dance
    As lang's I dow!   can

Now comes the *sax an' twentieth* simmer,   six, summer
I've seen the bud upo' the timmer,   wood
Still persecuted by the limmer   jade
    Frae year to year;
But yet, despite the kittle kimmer,   fickle woman
60   I, *Rob*, am here.

Do ye envy the *city-gent*,
Behint a kist to lie an' sklent,   counter, squint greedily
Or purse-proud, big wi' cent per cent,

An' muckle wame, *big belly*
In some bit *Brugh* to represent *small burgh*
A *Baillie's* name? *magistrate's*

Or is't the paughty, feudal *Thane*, *haughty*
Wi' ruffl'd sark an' glancin cane, *shirt*
Wha thinks himsel nae *sheep-shank bane*, *sheep-leg bone*
70   But lordly stalks,
While caps an' bonnets aff are taen,
As by he walks?

'O Thou wha gies us each guid gift!
Gie me o' *wit* an' *sense* a lift, *load*
Then turn me, if *Thou* please, *adrift*,
Thro' Scotland wide;
Wi' *cits* nor *lairds* I wadna shift, *townsmen, change places*
In a' their pride!'

Were this the *charter* of our state,
80 'On pain o' *hell* be rich an' great,'
Damnation then would be our fate,
Beyond remead; *remedy*
But, thanks to *Heav'n*, that's no the gate *way*
We learn our *creed*.

For thus the royal *Mandate* ran,
When first the human race began,
'The social, friendly, honest man,
Whate'er he be,
Tis *he* fulfils *great Nature's plan*,
90   And none but *he*.'

O *Mandate*, glorious and divine!
The followers o' the ragged Nine,
Poor, thoughtless devils! yet may shine
In glorious light,
While sordid sons o' Mammon's line
Are dark as night!

Tho' here they scrape, an' squeeze, an' growl,
Their worthless nievefu' of a *soul*,   fistful
May in some *future carcase* howl,
100   The forest's fright;
Or in some day-detesting *owl*
                    May shun the light.

Then may L*****K and B**** arise,
To reach their native, kindred skies,
And *sing* their pleasures, hopes an' joys,
                    In some mild sphere,
Still closer knit in friendship's ties
                    Each passing year!

TO W. S*****N, OCHILTREE

May —— 1785

I Gat your letter, winsome Willie;
Wi' gratefu' heart I thank you brawlie;   heartily
Tho' I maun say't, I wad be silly,
            An' unco vain,
Should I believe, my coaxin billie,   fellow
                    Your flatterin strain.

But I'se believe ye kindly meant it,   I'll
I sud be laith to think ye hinted   should, loath
Ironic satire, sidelins sklented,   sideways directed
10   On my poor Musie;   little Muse
Tho' in sic phraisin terms ye've penn'd it,   extravagant
                    I scarce excuse ye.

My senses wad be in a creel,   whirl
Should I but dare a *hope* to speel,   climb
Wi' *Allan*, or wi' *Gilbertfield*,
                    The braes o' fame;   slopes
Or *Ferguson*, the writer-chiel,   lawyer-chap
                    A deathless name.

(O *Ferguson!* thy glorious *parts*,
20   Ill-suited *law's* dry, musty arts!
My curse upon your whunstane hearts,   whinstone
         Ye Enbrugh Gentry!   Edinburgh
The tythe o' what ye waste at *cartes*   tenth
         Wad stow'd his pantry!)   stored

Yet when a tale comes i' my head,
Or lasses gie my heart a screed,   rent
As whiles they're like to be my dead,   death
         (O sad disease!)
I kittle up my *rustic reed*;   tickle/rouse
30   It gies me ease.

Auld COILA, now, may fidge fu' fain,   tingle with delight
She's gotten *Bardies* o' her ain,   own
Chiels wha their chanters winna hain,   fellows, will not spare
         But tune their lays,
Till echoes a' resound again
         Her weel-sung praise.

Nae *Poet* thought her worth his while,
To set her name in measur'd style;
She lay like some unkend-of isle
40   Beside *New Holland*,   Australia
Or whare wild-meeting oceans *boil*
         Besouth *Magellan*.   south of

Ramsay an' famous *Ferguson*
Gied *Forth* an' *Tay* a lift aboon;   up
Yarrow an' *Tweed*, to monie a tune,
         Owre Scotland rings,
While *Irwin, Lugar, Aire* an' *Doon*,
         Naebody sings.

Th' *Ilissus, Tiber, Thames* an' *Seine*,
50   Glide sweet in monie a tunefu' line;
But *Willie* set your fit to mine,   foot

An' cock your crest,   *hold up*
We'll gar our streams an' burnies shine   *make, streamlets*
     Up wi' the best.

We'll sing auld COILA'S plains an' fells,
Her moors red-brown wi' heather bells,
Her banks an' braes, her dens an' dells,   *hillsides*
     Where glorious WALLACE
Aft bure the gree, as story tells,   *bore off the prize*
60   Frae Suthron billies.   *Englishmen*

At WALLACE' name, what Scottish blood,
But boils up in a spring-tide flood!
Oft have our fearless fathers strode
     By WALLACE' side,
Still pressing onward, red-wat-shod,   *shod with wet blood*
     Or glorious dy'd!

O sweet are COILA'S haughs an' woods,   *hollows*
When lintwhites chant amang the buds,   *linnets*
And jinkin hares, in amorous whids,   *sporting, gambols*
70   Their loves enjoy,
While thro' the braes the cushat croods   *wood-pigeon, coos*
     With wailfu' cry!

Ev'n winter bleak has charms to me,
When winds rave thro' the naked tree;
Or frosts on hills of *Ochiltree*
     Are hoary gray;
Or blinding drifts wild-furious flee,
     Dark'ning the day!

O NATURE! a' thy shews an' forms
80 To feeling, pensive hearts hae charms!
Whether the Summer kindly warms,
     Wi' life an' light,
Or Winter howls, in gusty storms,
     The lang, dark night!

The *Muse*, nae *Poet* ever fand her,   found
Till by himsel he learn'd to wander,
Adown some trottin burn's meander,
      An' no think lang;
O sweet, to stray an' pensive ponder
90   A heart-felt sang!

The warly race may drudge an' drive,   worldly
Hog-shouther, jundie, stretch an' strive,   push, use elbows
Let me fair NATURE'S face descrive,   describe
      And I, wi' pleasure,
Shall let the busy, grumbling hive
      Bum owre their treasure.   boast

Fareweel, 'my rhyme-composing' brither!   brother
We've been owre lang unkenn'd to ither:
Now let us lay our heads thegither,
100   In love fraternal:
May *Envy* wallop in a tether,   be hanged, noose
      Black fiend, infernal!

While Highlandmen hate tolls an' taxes;
While moorlan herds like guid, fat braxies;   dead sheep
While Terra firma, on her axis,
      Diurnal turns,
Count on a friend, in faith an' practice,
      In ROBERT BURNS.

POSTSCRIPT

My memory's no worth a preen;   pin
110 I had amaist forgotten clean,
Ye bad me write you what they mean
      By this *new-light*,*
'Bout which our *herds* sae aft hae been   shepherds
      Maist like to fight.

* A cant-term for those religious opinions, which Dr Taylor of Norwich has defended so strenuously.

In days when mankind were but callans,   striplings
At *Grammar, Logic,* an' sic talents,
They took nae pains their speech to balance,
   Or rules to gie,
But spak their thoughts in plain, braid lallans,   vernacular Lowland
   Scots
120   Like you or me.

In thae auld times, they thought the *Moon,*   those
Just like a sark, or pair o' shoon,   shirt, shoes
Woor by degrees, till her last roon   wore out, round
   Gaed past their viewin,
An' shortly after she was done
   They gat a new ane.

This past for certain, undisputed;
It ne'er cam i' their heads to doubt it,
Till chiels gat up an' wad confute it,   fellows
130   An' ca'd it wrang;   wrong
An' muckle din there was about it,
   Baith loud an' lang.

Some *herds,* weel learn'd upo' the beuk,   book
Wad threap auld folk the thing misteuk;   insist, mistook
For 'twas the *auld moon* turn'd a newk   corner
   An' out o' sight,
An' backlins-comin, to the leuk,   backwards–, look
   She grew mair bright.

This was deny'd, it was affirm'd;
140 The *herds* an' *hissels* were alarm'd;   flocks
The rev'rend gray-beards rav'd an' storm'd,
   That beardless laddies   boys
Should think they better were inform'd,
   Than their auld daddies.

Frae less to mair it gaed to sticks;
Frae words an' aiths to clours an' nicks;   oaths, bumps
An' monie a fallow gat his licks,   punishment

Wi' hearty crunt;   blow
An' some, to learn them for their tricks,   teach
150   Were hang'd an' brunt.   burned

This game was play'd in monie lands,
An' *auld-light* caddies bure sic hands,   rascals, bore
That faith, the *youngsters* took the sands   fled
        Wi' nimble shanks,
Till *Lairds* forbad, by strict commands,
        Sic bluidy pranks.

But *new-light herds* gat sic a cowe,   trouncing
Folk thought them ruin'd stick-an-stowe,   utterly
Till now amaist on ev'ry *knowe*   hillock
160   Ye'll find ane plac'd;
An' some, their *New-light* fair avow,
        Just quite barefac'd.

Nae doubt the *auld-light flocks* are bleatan;
Their zealous *herds* are vex'd an' sweatan;
Mysel, I've ev'n seen them greetan   weeping
        Wi' girnan spite,   complaining
To hear the *Moon* sae sadly lie'd on
        By word an' write.

But shortly they will cowe the louns!   scare, rogues
170 Some *auld-light herds* in neebor towns   neighbouring
Are mind't, in things they ca' *balloons*,
        To tak a flight,
An' stay ae month amang the *Moons*
        An' see them right.

Guid observation they will gie them;
An' when the *auld Moon's* gaun to le'ae them,   leave
The hindmost *shaird*, they'll fetch it wi' them,   shard
        Just i' their pouch,   pocket
An' when the *new-light* billies see them,
180   I think they'll crouch!

Sae, ye observe that a' this clatter
Is naething but a 'moonshine matter;'
But tho' dull *prose-folk* latin splatter
    In logic tulzie,   squabble
I hope we, *Bardies*, ken some better
      Than mind sic brulzie.   brawl.

EPISTLE TO J. R******,

ENCLOSING SOME POEMS

O Rough, rude, ready-witted R******,
The wale o' cocks for fun an' drinkin!   choice
There's monie godly folks are thinkin,
    Your *dreams** an' tricks
Will send you, Korah-like, a sinkin,
      Straught to auld Nick's.   straight, Hell

Ye hae sae monie cracks an' cants,   songs, merry tales
And in your wicked, druken rants,   drunken, merry-making
Ye mak a devil o' the *Saunts*,   'Saints'/Elect
10   An' fill them fou;   make, drunk
And then their failings, flaws an' wants,
      Are a' seen thro'.

Hypocrisy, in mercy spare it!
That *holy robe*, O dinna tear it!   do not
Spare't for their sakes wha aften wear it,
    The lads in *black*;
But your curst wit, when it comes near it,
      Rives't aff their back.   tears

Think, wicked Sinner, wha ye're skaithing: hurting
20 It's just the *Blue-gown* badge an' claithing, clothing
O' Saunts; tak that, ye lea'e them naething, leave

---

* A certain humorous *dream* of his was then making a noise in the world.

>   To ken them by,
> Frae ony unregenerate Heathen,
>   Like you or I.

> I've sent you here, some rhymin ware,
> A' that I bargain'd for, an' mair;
> Sae when ye hae an hour to spare,
>   I will expect,
> Yon *Sang** ye'll sen't, wi' cannie care,   send it, discreet
> 30   And no neglect.

> Tho' faith, sma' heart hae I to sing!
> My Muse dow scarcely spread her wing: dares
> I've play'd mysel a bonie *spring*,   tune
>   An' *danc'd* my fill!
> I'd better gaen an' sair't the king,   served
>   At Bunker's hill.

> 'Twas ae night lately, in my fun,
> I gaed a rovin wi' the gun,
> An' brought a *Paitrick* to the *grun'*,   partridge, ground
> 40   A bonie *hen*,
> And, as the twilight was begun,
>   Thought nane wad ken.

> The poor, wee thing was *little hurt*;
> I *straiket* it a wee for sport,   stroked a little
> Ne'er thinkan they wad fash me for't;   trouble
>   But, Deil-ma-care!   Devil-me-care
> Somebody tells the *Poacher-Court*,   Kirk Session
>   The hale affair.   whole

> Some auld, us'd hands had taen a note,   experienced
> 50 That *sic a hen* had got a *shot*;   such and such
> I was suspected for the plot;
>   I scorn'd to lie;

* A *Song* he had promised the Author.

So gat the whissle o' my groat,   lost my money
   An' pay't the *fee*.

But by my *gun*, o' guns the wale,   pick
An' by my *pouther* an' my *hail*,   powder, shot
An' by my *hen*, an' by her *tail*,
   I vow an' swear!
The *Game* shall Pay, owre moor an' *dail*,   dale
60   For this, niest year.   next

As soon's the *clockin-time* is by,   hatching, over
An' the *wee powts* begun to cry,   chicks
L—d, I'se hae sportin by an' by,   I'll have
   For my *gowd guinea*;   gold
Tho' I should herd the *buckskin* kye   American cattle
   For't, in Virginia!

Trowth, they had muckle for to blame!
'Twas neither broken wing nor limb,
But twa-three *draps* about the *wame*   drops, womb
70   Scarce thro' the *feathers*;
An' baith a *yellow George* to claim,   guinea
   An' *thole* their *blethers*!   endure, nonsense

It pits me ay as mad's a hare;   puts
So I can rhyme nor write nae mair;
But *pennyworths* again is fair,
   When time's expedient:
Meanwhile I am, respected Sir,
   Your most obedient.

SONG

Tune, Corn rigs are bonie

I

IT was upon a Lammas night,
   When corn rigs are bonie,   ridges
Beneath the moon's unclouded light,
   I held awa to Annie: took my way
The time flew by, wi' tentless head,   careless
   Till 'tween the late and early;
Wi' sma' persuasion she agreed,
   To see me thro' the barley.

II

The sky was blue, the wind was still,
10   The moon was shining clearly;
I set her down, wi' right good will,
   Amang the rigs o' barley:
I ken't her heart was a' my ain;   own
   I lov'd her most sincerely;
I kiss'd her owre and owre again,
   Amang the rigs o' barley.

III

I lock'd her in my fond embrace;
   Her heart was beating rarely:
My blessings on that happy place,
20   Amang the rigs o' barley!
But by the moon and stars so bright,
   That shone that night so clearly!
She ay shall bless that happy night,
   Amang the rigs o' barley.

IV

I hae been blythe wi' Comrades dear;
   I hae been merry drinking;
I hae been joyfu' gath'rin gear;   money/property
   I hae been happy thinking;

But a' the pleasures e'er I saw,
30   Tho' three times doubl'd fairly,
That happy night was worth them a',
     Amang the rigs o' barley.

CHORUS

Corn rigs, an' barley rigs,
     An' corn rigs are bonie:
I'll ne'er forget that happy night,
     Amang the rigs wi' Annie.

SONG,
COMPOSED IN AUGUST

Tune, I had a horse, I had nae mair

I

NOW westlin winds, and slaught'ring guns   westerly
     Bring Autumn's pleasant weather;
And the moorcock springs, on whirring wings,
     Amang the blooming heather:
Now waving grain, wide o'er the plain,
     Delights the weary Farmer;
And the moon shines bright, when I rove at night,
     To muse upon my Charmer.

II

The Partridge loves the fruitful fells;
10   The Plover loves the mountains;
The Woodcock haunts the lonely dells;
     The soaring Hern the fountains:
Thro' lofty groves, the Cushat roves,   wood-pigeon
     The path of man to shun it;
The hazel bush o'erhangs the Thrush,
     The spreading thorn the Linnet.

III

Thus ev'ry kind their pleasure find,
    The savage and the tender;
Some social join, and leagues combine;
20   Some solitary wander:
Avaunt, away! the cruel sway,
    Tyrannic man's dominion;
The Sportsman's joy, the murd'ring cry,
    The flutt'ring, gory pinion!

IV

But PEGGY dear, the ev'ning's clear,
    Thick flies the skimming Swallow;
The sky is blue, the fields in view,
    All fading-green and yellow:
Come let us stray our gladsome way,
30   And view the charms of Nature;
The rustling corn, the fruited thorn,
    And ev'ry happy creature.

V

We'll gently walk, and sweetly talk,
    Till the silent moon shine clearly;
I'll grasp thy waist, and fondly prest,
    Swear how I love thee dearly:
Not vernal show'rs to budding flow'rs,
    Not Autumn to the Farmer,
So dear can be, as thou to me,
40   My fair, my lovely Charmer!

SONG

Tune, Gilderoy

I

FROM thee, ELIZA, I must go,
   And from my native shore:
The cruel fates between us throw
   A boundless ocean's roar;
But boundless oceans, roaring wide,
   Between my Love and me,
They never, never can divide
   My heart and soul from thee.

II

Farewell, farewell, ELIZA dear,
10   The maid that I adore!
A boding voice is in mine ear,
   We part to meet no more!
But the latest throb that leaves my heart,
   While Death stands victor by,
That throb, ELIZA, is thy part,
   And thine that latest sigh!

THE FAREWELL

To the Brethren of St. James's Lodge, Tarbolton

Tune, Goodnight and joy be wi' you a'

I

ADIEU! a heart-warm, fond adieu!
   Dear brothers of the *mystic tye*!
Ye favored, *enlighten'd* Few,
   Companions of my social joy!

Tho' I to foreign lands must hie,
    Pursuing Fortune's slidd'ry ba',   slippery ball
With melting heart, and brimful eye,
    I'll mind you still, tho' far awa.   remember

II

Oft have I met your social Band,
10   And spent the chearful, festive night;
Oft, honor'd with supreme command,
    Presided o'er the *Sons of light*:
And by that *Hieroglyphic* bright,
    Which none but *Craftsmen* ever saw!
Strong Mem'ry on my heart shall write
    Those happy scenes when far awa!

III

May Freedom, Harmony and Love
    Unite you in the *grand Design*,
Beneath th' Omniscient Eye above,
20   The glorious ARCHITECT Divine!
That you may keep th' *unerring line*,
    Still rising by the *plummet's law*,
Till *Order* bright, completely shine,
    Shall be my Pray'r when far awa.

IV

And YOU, farewell! whose merits claim,
    Justly that *highest badge* to wear!
Heav'n bless your honor'd, noble Name,
    To MASONRY and SCOTIA dear!
A last request, permit me here,
30   When yearly ye assemble a',
One *round*, I ask it with a *tear*,
    To him, *the Bard, that's far awa*.

EPITAPH ON A HENPECKED COUNTRY SQUIRE

As father Adam first was fool'd,
   A case that's still too common,
Here lyes a man a woman rul'd,
   The devil rul'd the woman.

EPIGRAM ON SAID OCCASION

O Death, hadst thou but spar'd his life,
   Whom we, this day, lament!
We freely wad exchang'd the *wife*,
   An' a' been weel content.

Ev'n as he is, cauld in his graff,   grave
   The *swap* we yet will do't;
Tak thou the Carline's carcase aff,   old woman's
   Thou'se get the *saul o' boot*.   thou'll

ANOTHER

One Queen Artemisa, as old stories tell,
When depriv'd of her husband she loved so well,
In respect for the love and affection he'd show'd her,
She reduc'd him to dust, and she drank up the Powder.

But Queen N**********, of a diff'rent complexion,   [Netherplace]
When call'd on to order the fun'ral direction,
Would have *eat* her dead lord, on a slender pretence,
Not to show her respect, but – *to save the expence*.

EPITAPHS

ON A CELEBRATED RULING ELDER

Here Sowter **** in Death does sleep;   [Hood]
   To H—ll, if he's gane thither,
Satan, gie him thy gear to keep,   money
   He'll haud it weel thegither.   hold

ON A NOISY POLEMIC

Below thir stanes lie Jamie's banes;   these stones, bones
   O Death, it's my opinion,
Thou ne'er took such a bleth'ran b—tch,   talkative
   Into thy dark dominion!

ON WEE JOHNIE

Hic jacet wee *Johnie*

Whoe'er thou art, O reader, know,
   That Death has murder'd Johnie;
An' here his *body* lies fu' low——   very
   For *saul* he ne'er had ony.   soul

FOR THE AUTHOR'S FATHER

O ye whose cheek the tear of pity stains,
   Draw near with pious rev'rence and attend!
Here lie the loving Husband's dear remains,
   The tender Father, and the gen'rous Friend.

The pitying Heart that felt for human Woe;
   The dauntless heart that fear'd no human Pride;
The Friend of Man, to vice alone a foe,
   'For ev'n his failings lean'd to Virtue's side.*'

* Goldsmith

For R. A. Esq;

Know thou, O stranger to the fame
Of this much lov'd, much honor'd name!
(For none that knew him need be told)
A warmer heart Death ne'er made cold.

For G. H. Esq;

The poor man weeps – here G—N sleeps,   [Gavin]
   Whom canting wretches blam'd:
But with *such as he*, where'er he be,
   May I be *sav'd* or *d—'d*!

A BARD'S EPITAPH

IS there a whim-inspir'd fool,
Owre fast for thought, owre hot for rule,   too
Owre blate to seek, owre proud to snool,   diffident, submit
     Let him draw near;   tamely
And o'er this grassy heap sing dool,   lament
     And drap a tear.   drop

Is there a Bard of rustic song,
Who, noteless, steals the crouds among,
That weekly this area throng,   churchyard
10   O, pass not by!
But with a frater-feeling strong,   brother-
     Here, heave a sigh.

Is there a man whose judgment clear,
Can others teach the course to steer,
Yet runs, himself, life's mad career,
     Wild as the wave,
Here pause – and thro' the starting tear,
     Survey this grave.

The poor Inhabitant below
20 Was quick to learn and wise to know,
And keenly felt the friendly glow,
And *softer flame*;
But thoughtless follies laid him low,
And stain'd his name!

Reader attend – whether thy soul
Soars fancy's flights beyond the pole,
Or darkling grubs this earthly hole,
In low pursuit,
Know, prudent, cautious, *self-controul*
30 Is Wisdom's root.

Notes

The Twa Dogs (p. 1). Drafted probably by November 1785, completed by mid-February 1786 (Burns to John Richmond, 17 February 1786; Richmond, 1765–1846, was one of Burns's intimates from the Mauchline period, a lawyer's clerk first in Gavin Hamilton's office there and later in Edinburgh). Burns's brother Gilbert explained that the poet's dog Luath, a great favourite, had been 'killed by the wanton cruelty of some person' the night before their father died (13 February 1784). 'Robert said to me, that he should like to confer such immortality as he could bestow upon his old friend *Luath*, and that he had a great mind to introduce something into the book under the title of *Stanzas to the Memory of a quadruped Friend*; but this plan was given up for the tale as it now stands. Caesar was merely the creature of the poet's imagination.'

Burns knew Fergusson's satirical dialogue poem 'Mutual Complaint of Plainstanes and Causey [pavement and street] in their Mother-tongue' (1773), written, like this poem, in octosyllabic couplets. With the example of Fergusson's deftly rendered colloquial Scots speech in mind, he has created a highly original form of social satire, using canine 'characters' to express pointed criticism. Fergusson has no such animal creations as Burns: indeed, only the Fables of the 15th-century poet Robert Henryson offer anything in Lowland Scots comparable to the astonishingly authentic blend of animal and human characteristics found in Caesar and Luath.

Part of the secret of Burns's success lies in the strategic skill with which he shows Caesar, the rich man's Newfoundland, kept as a pet, to be no stand-offish snob with his nose in the air, but on the contrary a willing companion for the 'gash an' faithfu' *tyke*' Luath, ready to share with him dogs' interests – and to talk – on equal terms. Not only is Caesar's freedom from class pretension in itself a means of commenting on the pettiness of human divisions. His genial outlook wins the goodwill of the reader: he is no biased observer of the life of the gentry, but instead a reliable witness, who can be trusted completely. His revelations carry weight therefore, and when he offers his summing-up, the tone of fair and deliberate judgment damns the life-style of the well-to-do much more effectively than a less carefully dramatized argument could possibly do:

> There's some exceptions, man an' woman;
> But this is Gentry's life in common.

2. COIL: Kyle, Burns's native, middle district of Ayrshire (cf. 'The Vision'). 'King Kyle' was the land within this district between the Ayr and the Doon.

11. some place far abroad: Newfoundland. 'A large breed of dog, noted for its sagacity, good temper, strength...' (*OED*), introduced to Britain in the 18th century.

27. in *Highland Sang*: 'Cuchullin's dog in Ossian's Fingal' (footnote by Burns). Controversy had raged for twenty years over James Macpherson's claim that *Fingal* (1762) was a translation of 'an ancient Epic'. Dr Johnson agreed with David Hume's comment that 'he would not believe the authenticity of *Fingal*, though fifty barearsed highlanders should swear it'.

51. racked rents: Rents in Ayrshire rose sharply in the agrarian revolution, some landlords exploiting the situation very unfairly.

65. Our *Whipper-in*: Hugh Andrew, who served Hugh Montgomerie of Coilsfield, Tarbolton.

96. a *factor*'s snash: 'My father's generous Master died [Provost Fergusson, in 1769]; the farm [Mount Oliphant] proved a ruinous bargain; and, to clench the curse, we fell into the hands of a Factor who sat for the picture I have drawn of one in my Tale of two dogs ... my indignation yet boils at the recollection of the scoundrel tyrant's insolent, threatening epistles' (Burns to Dr John Moore, 2 August 1787, *Letters* I. 136–7).

119. *patronage* an' *priests*: The Patronage Act of 1712 had reasserted the rights of lay patrons (usually local landowners) to appoint ministers to parishes of the Church of Scotland; but many people fiercely resisted this, believing that the right should lie instead with congregations. Another point of contention concerned the theological outlook of ministers, who were sometimes categorized – according to their beliefs – as 'Auld Licht' (strictly orthodox) or 'New Licht' (liberal).

181. breakin o' their timmer: The common people living on the land were often bitterly opposed to the large-scale tree planting which went on in the second half of the 18th century under the influence of 'improving' lairds. Saplings and young trees planted in country estates were sometimes destroyed under cover of darkness.

Scotch Drink (p. 9). Written between November 1785 and mid-February 1786 (letter to John Richmond, 17 February 1786). On 20 March 1786 Burns

wrote to his friend Robert Muir, wine-merchant in Kilmarnock: 'I here
inclose my SCOTCH DRINK, and "may the — follow with a blessing for
your edification". – I hope, sometime before we have the Gowk [cuckoo], to
have the pleasure of seeing you, at Kilm^k; when I intend we shall have a gill
between us, in a Mutchkin-stoup; which will be a great comfort and
consolation . . .'; (*Letters* I. 29). Fergusson's poem 'Caller Water' is Burns's
precedent for using the 6–line 'Standart Habby' stanza (see p.34) in a poem
celebrating the rejection of wine for another kind of drink. Compare with
the opening of 'Scotch Drink', 'Caller Water', ll. 19–24:

> The fuddlin' Bardies now–a–days
> Rin *maukin*–mad in Bacchus' praise,
> And limp and stoiter thro' their lays
>> *Anacreontic,*
> While each his sea of wine displays
>> As big's the Pontic.

17. *John Barleycorn:* The grain from which malt liquor is made.
28. oil'd by thee: cf. Ramsay, 'Epistle to Robert Yarde', lls. 105–8:

> A cheerfu' Bottle sooths the Mind,
> Gars Carles grow canty, free and kind;
> Defeats our Care, and hales our Strife,
> And brawly oyls the Wheels of Life.

41. pirratch: This form has manuscript authority, though Burns
    changed it to the more usual *parritch* in his 1787 edition.
70. Wae worth . . . Gies famous sport.: Toned down in 1787 to:

> Wae worth the name!
> Nae Howdie [midwife] gets a social night,
>> Or plack [coin] frae them.

84. spier her price . . . *Brandy*, burnan trash!: In Fergusson's 'A Drink
    Eclogue', ll. 63–4, whisky says to brandy:

> For now our Gentles gabbs are grown sae nice,
> At thee they toot, an' never speer my price.

109. Thee, *Ferintosh*! O sadly lost!: Whisky distilled at Ferintosh on the
     Cromarty Firth had been exempt from duty since 1695 in repara-
     tion for damage (caused in 1689 by the Jacobites) to the estates of
     Forbes of Culloden, who owned the distillery. In 1785 the exemption
     was withdrawn. Although more than £20,000 was paid in compen-
     sation, the price of whisky rose. Burns's poem reflects the continuing
     keen interest in the subject in Scotland from the consumer's
     viewpoint.
115. curst horse–leeches o' th'Excise: Ironical, considering that Burns
     was later to accept employment himself as an exciseman.

The Author's Earnest Cry and Prayer (p. 13). A note in the 1787 edition indicates the occasion for this poem, 'before the Act anent the Scotch Distilleries, of session 1786; for which Scotland and the Author return their most grateful thanks'. Burns's plea to the Scottish MPs at Westminster was thus highly topical. Feelings had been running high in Scotland since the passing of the Wash Act in 1784, which it was alleged discriminated against Scottish distillers ('that curst restriction', l.15). There were many illicit stills in Scotland at this period, and excisemen who made a practice of seizing stills were very unpopular (cf. 'Scotch Drink', l.115). The legislation of 1786 taxed distillers on the capacity of their stills, and regulated whisky sales between Scotland and England.

Title: cf. 2 *Chronicles* 6:19: '. . . hearken unto the cry and the prayer which thy servant prayeth before thee'.

Epigraph: Burns parodies *Paradise Lost*, ix, 896, 900:

        O fairest of creation! last and best . . .

        How art thou lost . . .

  1. YE *Irish lords*: Certain Irish lords had Scottish seats in Parliament, while the eldest sons of Scottish peers were ineligible.

 15. that curst restriction: The Wash Act of 1784 had reduced the profits of Scottish distillers.

 19. yon PREMIER YOUTH: William Pitt the Younger (b. 1759), prime minister since 1784.

 39. d—mn'd Excise-men: Excisemen were engaged in the mid-1780s in a campaign against illicit whisky stills. In view of Burns's later career in the Excise, his comments on excisemen in this poem are charged with unconscious irony.

 57. like MONTGOMERIES fight: The Earls of Eglinton. Over the centuries many members of this Ayrshire family had borne arms with distinction. After a long military career, Archibald, the eleventh Earl (1726–96), was appointed governor of Edinburgh Castle in 1782.

 58. gab like BOSWEll: James Boswell (1740–95), advocate, biographer of Samuel Johnson, and Laird of Auchinleck in Ayrshire; at this time active in Ayrshire politics. In 1788 Burns sought an introduction, explaining to Bruce Campbell (a mutual acquaintance), 'as I had the honor of drawing my first breath almost in the same Parish with Mr Boswell, my Pride plumes itself on the connection' (letter of 13 November 1788). Boswell endorsed his letter, 'Mr Robert Burns the Poet expressing very high sentiments of me', but he did not invite Burns to meet him.

 71. Saint Stephen's wa's: St Stephen's chapel in the palace of Westminster, the House of Commons.

 73. *Dempster*: 'Honest George' Dempster (1732–1818), Whig MP for Forfar Burghs, and a noted agricultural improver.

74. *Kilkerran*: Sir Adam Fergusson of Kilkerran, third baronet (1733–1814), MP for Ayrshire 1774–84 and 1790–96; described as 'aith–detesting' perhaps because of his reported way of rebuking his children with the words, 'Dinna think that because I'm no swearin I'm no angry.'

76. *Graham*: James Graham (1755–1836), later third Duke of Montrose. One of Pitt's ministers in 1783, he eventually became Lord Justice-General. Noted for his 'ready elocution'.

78. *Dundas*: Henry Dundas (1742–1811), at this time MP for Midlothian and Treasurer of the Navy under Pitt; a man of exceptional political influence, especially in Scotland.

79. *Erskine*: Thomas Erskine (1750–1823), son of the tenth Earl of Erskine, MP for Portsmouth, 1783, and subsequently Lord Chancellor; 'an honourable politician, an enthusiast for liberty' (*DNB*).

80. Campbels, *Frederic* an' *Ilay*: Lord Frederick Campbell (1736–1816), third son of the fourth Duke of Argyll, and at this time an MP for Argyll; and Sir Ilay Campbell (1734–1823), member for the Glasgow burghs from 1784, and Lord Advocate.

81. Livistone: Sir William Cuninghame of Milncraig, Ayrshire, and Livingston in Linlithgow; MP for Linlithgow 1774–90.

92. *lost Militia*: In 1782 a militia bill for Scotland, which would have allowed for enlistment from the militia into the army, was opposed by the Scottish representatives at Westminster.

109. *Charlie Fox*: Charles James Fox (1749–1806), Whig leader and gifted rival of Pitt; a notorious gambler and womanizer.

115. *Boconnock's*: The prime minister was a grandson of Robert Pitt of Boconnoc in Cornwall.

119. tea an' winnocks: In an effort to curb smuggling, Pitt's Commutation Act of 1784 slashed the import duty on tea, making up for the loss of revenue by a tax on windows in houses.

126. The *Coalition*: The Fox-North administration of 1783.

133. FIVE AND FORTY: The Scottish representatives in the Commons.

142. St *Jamie's*: Westminster.

176. raise a philosophic reek: Many 18th-century writers argued that climate affected character. Burns may have been familiar with Montesquieu's view, as quoted by Henry Mackenzie in the *Mirror* (27 March 1779), 'difference of climate is the chief, or the only cause of the difference of national characters'.

183–6. Till . . . *dram*!: Burns amended the ending in a holograph note in a copy of his 1793 edition, now in the Huntington Library, to read:

> Till when ye speak, ye aiblins blether;
>   Yet deil-mak-matter!
> FREEDOM and WHISKY gang thegither,
>   Tak aff your whitter.

The Holy Fair (p. 20). 'Composed in 1785' (note by Burns on the Kilmarnock MS), probably after the Mauchline annual Communion, held on the second Sunday in August. Mauchline had only 400 communicant church members, but it is known that in 1786 no fewer than 1,400 received the sacrament, and there is no reason to think such a number was unusual. A Holy Fair went on for several days before reaching its climax in the Communion service; people came from far and wide to hear the 'preachings'. Hence the pretext for communal involvement on the scale and of the boisterous sort described by Burns. In real life, as in Burns's poem, noisy rival factions supported 'Auld Licht' (evangelical) and 'New Licht' (moderate) preachers; hard drinking went on in Nanse Tinnock's tavern next to the churchyard; and many country-dwellers got into the habit of treating the series of religious meetings as a prelude to letting their hair down.

Burns's first aim is to amuse by creating a lively and convivial scene. His companion Fun, however, directs laughter specifically at Superstitition and Hypocrisy (stanzas 3 to 5). 'The Holy Fair' quickly becomes a social satire which turns on a series of contrasts between lofty pretensions and lowly performance, between loudly professed religious motives and actual human inclinations – which prove too strong to resist – to booze, quarrel, and fornicate.

Behind the poem lies a long tradition of Scottish vernacular verse, from the mediaeval 'brawl' poems 'Chrystis Kirk of the Grene' and 'Peblis to the Play' to Robert Fergusson's 'Leith Races' and 'Hallow-Fair'. Burns borrows his metrical form from Fergusson, and broadly keeps to the traditional combination of playful irony and vigorous social description. Certain details point to his also having read *A Letter from a Blacksmith to the Ministers and Elders of the Church of Scotland* (1759). However, 'The Holy Fair' displays a highly original thematic unity. Burns gives depth and meaning to the vividly rendered particulars which belong to his satirical celebration. His early 19th-century biographer J. G. Lockhart noted accurately that, with the publication of this poem, 'national manners were once more in the hands of a national poet'.

Title: 'Holy Fair is a common phrase in the West of Scotland for a
   sacramental occasion' (Burns, in his 1787 edition).
Epigraph: From a satire by Tom Brown directed against Jeremy Collier, *The
   Stage Beaux toss'd in a Blanket; or, Hypocrisie Alamode* (1704).
   5. GALSTON: A village a few miles north of Mossgiel.

37. My name is FUN: cf. Fergusson's account in 'Leith Races' of his meeting with Mirth, a 'laughing lass', whom he takes as his companion for the day (*Poems*, STS,ii,160–1).

41–5. to ********* *holy fair*: cf. 'Leith Races', ll. 37–45:

> A bargain be't, and, by my feggs,
> Gif ye will be my mate,
> Wi' you I'll screw the cheery pegs,
> Ye shanna find me blate;
> We'll reel an' ramble thro' the sands,
> And jeer wi' a' we meet . . .

cf. also Burns's 'Epistle to J. L*****k', ll. 103–6.

61. *sweet-milk cheese*: A special treat. 'The milk, the cheese, the butter were reserved by the thrifty housewife from the family with jealous care, that they might be converted into cash' (John Mitchell, DD, *Memories of Ayrshire about 1780*, ed. W. K. Dickson, Scottish History Society, Miscellany, vi, 1939, p. 272).

66. *black-bonnet*: The officiating elder wore a black cap of traditional design.

75. *racer Jess*: Janet Gibson, the half-witted daughter of 'Poosie Nansie' (Agnes Gibson), who kept a disreputable tavern in the Cowgate, Mauchline. Jess ran errands for her mother.

86. an *Elect* swatch: Amended in 1787 to 'a Chosen swatch'.

91. O happy is that man, an' blest!: Burns here quotes line 1 of verse 2 from the Scottish Metrical version of Psalm 146, which may be being sung even as the scene he describes is enacted.

102. ****** speels the holy door: Identified as 'Sawnie' in two manuscripts. Alexander Moodie (1728–99), minister of Riccarton from 1762, said once to have preached to his congregation on John 8:44, 'Ye are of your father the devil, and the lusts of your father ye will do.'

103. tidings o' s-lv-t-n: Changed in 1787 to 'tidings o' d-mn-t-n' after Dr Hugh Blair, minister of the High Kirk in Edinburgh and Professor of Rhetoric in Edinburgh University, had objected that the original 'gives just offence. The Author may easily contrive some other Rhyme in place of the word Salv—n.'

104. *Hornie*, as in ancient days: cf. Job 1:6, 'Now there was a day when the sons of God came to present themselves before the Lord, and Satan came also among them.'

116. cantharidian plaisters: Plasters of cantharides (Spanish fly), an aphrodisiac.

122. ***** opens out his cauld harangues: MS 'Geordie begins his . . .' George Smith (d. 1823), a 'New Licht' moderate, minister of Galston.

The preaching of such ministers was dismissed by the 'Auld Licht' evangelicals as insipid, mere morals without faith. Here, Smith's sermon sends off the godly in search of drink.

132. ANTONINE: Roman emperor and reformer.

138. *******, frae the water-fit: MS 'Willy'. Rev. William Peebles (1753–1826), of Newton-upon-Ayr, clerk of the Ayr Presbytery. Burns describes him in 'The Holy Tulzie' as 'shaul' (shallow). Peebles never forgave Burns, and in 1811 published verses scorning 'Burnomania', the rise of the Burns cult.

143. COMMON-SENSE: Traditionally identified as the poet's friend Dr John Mackenzie of Mauchline.

145. Wee ****** niest: MS 'M—R'. Alexander Miller, 'the assistant minister at St Michael's' (Burns, in a copy of the Kilmarnock edition); from 1788 minister of Kilmaurs, where his presentation by the Earl of Eglinton led to violent opposition from the congregation. Miller was short and very stout.

184. Black ******: John Russel (c.1740–1817), previously schoolmaster at Cromarty, ordained as minister at Kilmarnock in 1774; notorious for his severity of temper and doctrine.

188. 'Sauls does harrow': *Hamlet* I, v, 15ff., 'I could a Tale unfold . . . harrow up thy soul.'

226. *Clinkumbell*: The town-crier, bellman.

237. hearts o' stane: Burns plays boldly on Ezekiel 36:26: 'A new heart also will I give you, and a new spirit will I put within you: and I will take away the stony heart out of your flesh, and I will give you an heart of flesh.'

231. lasses strip their shoon . . . : Burns's way of ending 'The Holy Fair' shows that he has borrowed hints from Ramsay's addition to 'Chrystis Kirk of the Grene' (Ramsay, *Works*, STS, i, 73):

> And unko Wark that fell at E'en,
> Whan Lasses were haff winkin,
> They lost their Feet and baith their Een,
> And Maidenheads gae'd linkin
> Aff a' that Day.

Address to the Deil (p. 28). Written in the winter of 1785–6: Burns refers to it as completed in his letter to Richmond of 17 February 1786. While he has no exact model for a comic invocation of this degree of boldness, vernacular Scots tradition is rich in reductive humour concerning the supernatural – born in part out of fear. This humour is made the basis of his art in 'Address to the Deil'. Burns clearly enjoys taking a radically different attitude to his subject from Milton in *Paradise Lost*. The poem begins as an exercise in the medieval craft of 'flyting' or scolding in verse; but as it develops, it anticipates 'Halloween' and 'Tam o' Shanter' as an ironic portrayal of still powerful, though waning, popular beliefs. Burns calls the Devil by a series of familiar, disrespectful nicknames (Hornie, Nick, Clootie, Hangie), bringing him down to his own level and robbing him of dignity. He then goes on to enumerate traditional beliefs concerning the actions of the Devil and of his agents on earth, warlocks and witches, before gently dismissing Satan as an enemy whose measure he has taken.

The poem was more sexually explicit in manuscript, and also more personal, than appears from the printed version. Lines 61–6 originally contained a bawdy joke about a bridegroom interrupted in his love-making by evil spells:

> Thence, knots are coosten, spells contriv'd,
> An' the brisk bridegroom, newly wived
> Just at the kittle point arriv'd,
>> Fond, keen, an' croose,
> Is by some spitefu' jad depriv'd
>> O's warklum's use.

When Burns was revising his *Poems* for the 1787 Edinburgh edition, the critic Hugh Blair suggested that the (toned down) stanza printed in 1786 'had better be left out, as indecent': Burns did not act on this advice. A different motive had in 1786 led the poet to replace manuscript ll. 89–90 containing a direct tribute to Jean Armour:

> Langsyne, in Eden's happy scene,
> When strappin Edie's days were green,
> An' Eve was like my bonie Jean,
>> My dearest part,
> A dancin, sweet, young, handsome quean
>> Wi' guileless heart.

This change seems to have been made shortly before publication – by the summer of 1786 Burns was estranged from Jean. With regard to the stanza immediately following, there was certainly no love lost between Burns and Jean's father; and Burns may also have thought of 'Daddie' Auld, a minister friendly to the Armours, in the role of killjoy 'snick-drawing dog' driving Jean and himself out of Paradise.

Epigraph: *Paradise Lost*, i, 128–9. cf. letter to William Nicol of 18 June 1787, 'I have bought a pocket Milton, which I carry perpetually about with me, in order to study the sentiments – the dauntless magnanimity; the intrepid unyielding independance; the desperate daring, and noble defiance of hardship, in that great Personage, Satan.' (*Letters* I. 123).

1. O Thou: An echo of Pope's way of addressing Swift in *The Dunciad*, i, 19–20:

> O Thou! whatever title please thine ear,
> Dean, Drapier, Bickerstaff, or Gulliver!

2. Auld Hornie: Traditional Scottish nickname for the horned Devil. 'Nick' may be a form of Nicholas (reason obscure), while 'Clootie' means 'cloven-hoofed'.

19. roaring lion: 1 Peter 5:8, 'your adversary the devil, as a roaring lion, walketh about, seeking whom he may devour'.

21. strong-wing'd Tempest: Tradition had it that the Devil raised strong winds.

35. boortries: Elder trees were supposed to give protection against witchcraft.

45. stoor: 'sounding hollow, strong, and hoarse' (B).

50. ragweed: Witches were said to ride on many kinds of steed – animals, enchanted humans, ragwort, ash branches, or straws.

61. mystic knots: Knots devised in malice by witches.

63. *wark-lume*: According to a 17th-century tract, *Satan's Invisible World Discovered*, witches sometimes meddled with the weaver's craft. Burns uses the word with a sexual meaning.

69. *Water-kelpies*: Water-demons in the shape of horses, bent on drowning travellers (traditional in the Scottish Highlands). Burns wrote to Cunningham on 10 September 1792 of 'a Kelpie, haunting the ford, or ferry, in the starless night, mixing thy laughing yell with the howling of the storm' (*Letters* II. 145).

73. *Spunkies*: 'As for Willy and the Wisp, he is a fiery devil, and leads people off their road in order to drown them, for he sparks sometimes at our feet, and then turns before us with his candle, as if he were twa or three miles before us, many a good boat has Spunkie drown'd' (Dougal Graham, *History of Buckhaven in Fifeshire*, 1806).

79. When MASONS' mystic *word* an' *grip*: Burns refers to the Masonic password and handshake as having force to stir up the Devil in a storm; then by contrast to the tradition that a cock, cat, or other unchristened creature was needed in order to appease the Devil. A joke at the expense of Masons, including the poet himself.

85. Lang syne in EDEN'S bonie yard: cf. Fergusson, 'Caller Water', ll. 1-2 (*Poems*, STS, ii, 106):

> When father Adie first pat spade in
> The bonny yeard of antient Eden.

By July 1786 Burns was estranged from Jean Armour, and this stanza replaces one in the Kilmarnock MS (see introductory note, above).

91. snick-drawing: 'An auld sneck-drawer, one who, from long experience, has acquired a great degree of facility in accomplishing any artful purpose' (*Jamieson's Scots Dictionary*).

107. lows'd his ill-tongu'd, wicked *Scawl*: cf. Job 2: 8–10, 'Thou speakest as one of the foolish women speaketh.'
111. MICHAEL: cf. *Paradise Lost*, vi, 320, 'then Satan first knew pain . . .'
123–4. Ye aiblins might . . . hae a *stake*: cf. Sterne, *Tristram Shandy*, III, xi: 'I declare, quoth my uncle Toby, my heart would not let me curse the devil himself . . . But he is cursed and damned already, to all eternity, replied Dr Slop. I am sorry for it, quoth my uncle Toby.'

The Death and Dying Words of Poor Mailie (p. 32). Burns's first sustained poem in Scots, included in his First Commonplace Book in an entry dated June 1785, but written considerably earlier. According to his brother Gilbert, he had 'partly by way of frolic, bought a ewe and two lambs from a neighbour, and she was tethered in a field adjoining the house at Lochlea. He and I were going out with our teams, and our two younger brothers to drive for us, at mid-day, when Hugh Wilson, a curious-looking, awkward boy, clad in plaiding, came to us with much anxiety in his face, with the information that the ewe had entangled herself in the tether, and was lying in the ditch. Robert was much tickled with Huoc's appearance and postures on the occasion. Poor Mailie was set to rights, and when we returned from the plough in the evening he repeated to me her *Death and Dying Words* pretty much in the way they now stand.'

Poor Mailie's Elegy (p. 34). Written to accompany *The Death and Dying Words of Poor Mailie*, but possibly not until Burns had decided to publish his poems. Here he follows a very distinctive tradition of comic elegy in Scots, making use of the 6-line stanza employed by Robert Sempill of Beltrees in *The Life and Death of Habbie Simpson* in the late 17th century, and more recently by William Hamilton of Gilbertfield in his *Last Words of Bonny Heck, a Famous Greyhound*. Allan Ramsay, who named the verse form 'Standart Habby' after the first example above, had used it for familiar epistles, as well as for elegy. Fergusson continued this tradition; and Burns in turn widened the range of the stanza still further, handling it so often and with such success that it came to be known after his death as 'the Burns stanza'. See, for example, 'To J.S****' and 'The Vision'.

To J. S**** (p. 36). The first of seven verse-epistles included in *Poems, Chiefly in the Scottish Dialect*. Written when Burns had already decided to publish his poems, in the winter of 1785–6 . . .

> This while my notion's taen a sklent,
> To try my fate in guid, black *prent*. (ll. 37–8)

James Smith, six years younger than Burns, was the son of a merchant in Mauchline, and at this time was himself a draper there. Along with John Richmond and the poet, he was one of the self-styled 'Court of Equity', a 'ramstam' (l. 165) bachelor trio who met in the Whitefoord Arms Inn in Mauchline. Burns celebrated their rakish activities in a riotous mock-trial poem, 'The Court of Equity', which was not published in his lifetime. Smith proved a staunch friend to Burns during his troubles with Jean Armour's family. He worked for a time as a calico-printer in Linlithgow, subsequently emigrating to Jamaica, where he died young.

The poem follows the pattern established in Scots verse-epistles by Ramsay and Fergusson. Beginning with greetings and compliments to Smith, Burns moves on to discuss questions of mutual interest, before returning to a brief final salutation. A particularly lively passage explains Burns's reasons for rhyming (ll. 19-30). His colloquial Scots modulates into lightly accented English in the reflective central part of the poem (ll. 55–120); then he slips back into the vernacular.

14. scrimpet stature: This stanza, with its jest about Smith's diminutive stature, was a late addition to the poem in manuscript.

25. Some rhyme . . . : This much-quoted stanza replaced an earlier manuscript version:

> Some rhyme because they like to clash,
> An' gie a neebor's name a lash;
> An' some (vain thought) for needfu' cash;
> An' some for fame;
> For me, I string my dogg'rel trash
> For fun at hame.

133. DEMPSTER: George Dempster (1732–1818), Whig MP and agricultural improver. cf. 'The Author's Earnest Cry and Prayer', above, l. 73n.

A Dream (p. 42). The poet laureate, Thomas Warton, published a laudatory Pindaric Ode to mark the birthday of King George III on 4 June 1786. This incident must have provoked Burns to write almost at once his very different poem, 'A Dream', because his book was in print by the end of July. 'A Dream' was therefore in its content and allusions the most topical and up-to-date of all the poems included in the Kilmarnock volume. The convention Burns adopts, of free speech within an imagined dream framework, is a common one in satirical journalism of the Georgian period.

Burns's friend Mrs Dunlop advised him to omit 'A Dream' from the second edition of his *Poems*: 'numbers at London are learning Scots to read your book, but they don't like your Address to the King, and say it will hurt the sale of the rest' (letter of 26 February 1787, *Correspondence of Robert Burns and Mrs Dunlop*, ed. William Wallace (1898), pp. 11, 13). Burns rejected her suggestion, replying, 'You are right in your guesses that I am not very amenable to counsel . . . I set as little by kings, lords, clergy, critics, &c. as all these respectable Gentry do by my Bardship' (30 April 1787, *Letters* I. 108).

26. *ane* been better: Burns was a 'sentimental Jacobite', and believed that his father's family had been removed from their land in north-east Scotland because of their loyalty to the Jacobite Earl Marischal.

36. then did ae day: i.e. before the loss of the American colonies.

61. let nae *saving–fit*: A recent proposal had been made to cut down the size of the Navy.

67. gie her for dissection!: Surgeons were allowed, for dissection, the bodies of executed criminals.

79. to release Ye: Burns alludes glancingly to the fact that the Queen had already mothered a large family.

81. young Potentate o' W——: George, Prince of Wales (1762–1830), the future George IV, already a byword for extravagant living, matronly mistresses, and a love of gambling.

88. Diana's *pales*: The boundaries of Diana, goddess of the moon and of the hunt. cf. Shakespeare, *1 Henry IV*, I,ii,25.

89. *Charlie*: Charles James Fox, out-of-office Whig leader and gambling companion of the Prince of Wales.

100. right reverend O—— : Frederick, Duke of York (1763–1827), who while still an infant had been made Bishop of Osnaburg in Westphalia by George III. (Appointed Commander-in-Chief of the British Army in 1798, the Duke had to resign in 1809 as a result of scandal.)

109. royal TARRY–BREEKS: Prince William (1765–1837), later Duke of Clarence and King William IV. His name had recently been linked with that of Sarah Martin, daughter of the Commissioner of Portsmouth Dockyard.

118. Ye . . . bonie blossoms a': The daughters of the royal family were Charlotte (b.1766), Augusta (b.1768), Elizabeth (b.1770), Mary (b.1776), Sophia (b.1777), and Amelia (b.1783).

The Vision (p. 47). Probably written no earlier than August 1785, when Burns noted in his Commonplace Book his disappointment that, despite the varied natural beauty and historic achievements of Ayrshire, 'we have never had one Scotch Poet of any eminence'; then outlined his poetic ambition to 'make the fertile banks of Irvine, the romantic woodlands & sequestered scenes on Aire, and the heathy, mountainous source, & winding sweep of Doon emulate Tay, Forth, Ettrick, Tweed &c.', adding 'no young Poet, nor young Soldier's heart ever beat more fondly for fame than mine'. Burns celebrates different aspects of regional life with enthusiasm in 'The Vision', defining the modest but vital part which he himself is called on to play as 'rustic bard'. Coila watches benevolently over Kyle, Burns's native district of Ayrshire, as one of a force of tutelary spirits, rather as Ariel and other spirits protect humans in *The Rape of the Lock*. After the vernacular Scots opening, Coila speaks dignified English, the language of instruction in Burns's Scotland. Burns arranges the poem, as a note explains, in two 'duans' or sections, on the digressive model of James Macpherson. He owes a general debt in this poem – as does Wordsworth in *The Prelude* – to James Beattie's blank-verse poem 'The Minstrel' (1771–4), which describes how the process of growing up in a country environment inspires the thoughts and feelings of a young poet. The stanza form is 'Standart Habby'.

Additional stanzas existed in manuscript, and the poem was expanded in 1787.

2. their roaring play: Curling, an energetic game played on ice, is sometimes referred to as 'the roaring game'.

3. hunger'd Maukin: cf. Thomson, 'Winter', ll.257–62:

> The hare,
> Though timorous of heart . . .
> . . . the garden seeks,
> Urged on by fearless want.

55. 'hare-brain'd, sentimental trace': Burns quotes from own verse epistle 'To J. S****', l.157.

63. Bess: Elizabeth Paton, servant at Lochlea, bore Burns a child in May 1785, on whose behalf he made a settlement in 1786. Burns was estranged from Jean Armour when the Kilmarnock *Poems* appeared. In later editions he substituted 'Jean' for 'Bess'.

79–82. Doone . . . Irwine . . . Air: Rivers of Ayrshire.

86. An ancient BOROUGH: Ayr.

121. FULLARTON: William Fullarton (1754–1808), of Dundonald, had a varied career as politician, diplomat, and soldier in India before becoming one of the leading agricultural improvers in Ayrshire.

122. DEMPSTER: 'Honest George' Dempster (1732–1818), MP and agricultural improver.

123. BEATTIE: Dr James Beattie (1735–1803), Professor of Moral Philosophy in Aberdeen, author of an *Essay on the Nature and Immutability of Truth* criticizing Hume's scepticism, and poet of *The Minstrel: or, The Progress of Genius* (1771–4).

151. COILA my name: From Kyle, Burns's own district of Ayrshire, between Carrick to the south and Cunningham to the north.

153. once the *Campbells*: Burns's farm Mossgiel, leased from Gavin Hamilton, was part of the Loudoun estate, above the river Irvine to the east of Kilmarnock. The Earls of Loudoun were Campbells, and the Campbell connection went back to the 14th century.

199ff. Thou canst not learn . . .: Burns wrote to Dr John Moore in January 1787: 'my first ambition was, and still my strongest wish is, to please my Compeers, the rustic Inmates of the Hamlet, while ever-changing language and manners will allow me to be relished and understood . . . in a language where Pope and Churchill have raised the laugh, and Shenstone and Gray drawn the tear; where Thomson and Beattie have painted the landskip, and Littleton and Collins described the heart; I am not vain enough to hope for distinguished Poetic fame' (*Letters* I. 88).

213. *Potosi's mine*: silver, gold, and copper mines in Bolivia.

Halloween (p. 55). Probably written in the autumn of 1785: Burns revised and expanded before publication his accompanying footnote commentary on the Halloween rituals he describes in the poem. This is arguably the most thoroughgoing example of 'manners-painting' in the Kilmarnock edition. From start to finish, in both poem and notes, Burns presents a record of social customs in his part of Ayrshire, and explains the various traditions described with the zeal of a folklorist and antiquary. He writes, in part at least, specifically to interest outsiders in a world which he had known as an observer–participant.

It seems likely that he includes in this poem Ayrshire lore from his mother's family. 'Wee Jenny', mentioned in stanza 13, has been identified as his cousin Jenny Broun; likewise, the old woman who recalls 'as weel's yestreen' (l.128) a harvest-home which took place before 1715, may be modelled on a member of the extended family. It is also tempting to assume that the setting of the poem at Cassilis Downans (l.2), and mention of a place 'where three Lairds' lan's meet at a burn' (l.214) (as they did on the boundary of Mount Oliphant) specifically point to places remembered from Burns's boyhood. 'Halloween', however, is a composite picture. All that can safely be said is that personal memories played some part in the making of a poem which is designed to be an authentic and also humorous guide to Ayrshire Halloween traditions.

Epigraph: Goldsmith, *The Deserted Village*, ll. 251–4.

1. that *night*: Halloween, which marks the beginning of the winter half of the year, derives from the great winter feast of the pagan Celts, immediately followed since the 9th century by the Christian festival of All Saints. According to traditional belief in Scotland, spirits are abroad on the night before 1 November, and humans are then able, through use of the proper ritual customs, to ask what the future holds, especially with regard to marriage. The 'mischief night' element symbolizes the activities of the spirits.

5. *Colean*: Culzean Castle, Kirkoswald.

14. *Carrick*: The southern district of Ayrshire.

55. Guidwife's weel-hoordet *nits*: cf. John Mayne's poem, 'Halloween', published in Ruddiman's *Weekly Magazine*, November 1780:

> Plac'd at their head the gudewife sits,
> And deals round apples, pears, and nits . . .

96. for the *kiln*: Where a fire was lit to dry grain, especialy oats. Different types of corn-kiln are described by A. Fenton, in *Scottish Country Life* (1976), pp. 94–6. A common superstition was that there dwelt within the walled kiln, beneath the cross-beams, a 'kiln-carle', hostile when provoked. 'To wind the *blue clue* in the *killpot* on halloween, was a serious matter before Burns made the world laugh at it' (MacTaggart, *Gallovidian Encyclopaedia*, 1824, p.138).

109. Wee *Jenny*: Traditionally identified as Burns's cousin Jenny Broun (b. 1765). Burns may have stayed with the family at Kirkoswald in 1775.

118. Skelpie-limmer's-face: 'a technical term in female scolding' (B.). cf. the gudame's outlook in Fergusson's 'The Farmer's Ingle', l. 60ff.

127. The *Sherra-moor*: Battle of Sheriffmuir (1715), fought between the Earl of Mar's Jacobité troops and pro-Hanoverian forces under the Duke of Argyll.

133. a rantan *Kirn*: A time of celebration on farms. cf. 'The Twa Dogs', l.124.

139. Achmacalla: Probably a name invented for the rhyme.

156. *graip*: An iron-pronged dung-fork.

163. lord Lennox' march: Possibly 'Port Lennox', a march, included in Daniel Dow's *A Collection of Ancient Scots Music* (c.1783) and in

James Bowie's *A Collection of Strathspey Reels and Country Dances* (c.1789). Information kindly supplied by Peter Cooke, School of Scottish Studies, Edinburgh. Dr Cooke suggests that Burns may be 'having a little joke about antiquarians', since Dow's book was a specialized collection, primarily of historical interest.

201. he *faddom't thrice*: 'This incantation was performed by measuring or fathoming with the arms round a stack of oats or barley three times, against the sun' (W. Gregor, 1881).

214. *three Lairds' lan's met at a burn*: At Riddicks Moss Burn, the lands of Mount Oliphant, Rozelle and Pleasantfield met.

240. *Mar's-year*: The Earl of Mar led a Jacobite Rising in 1715.

248. *butter'd So'ns*: Sowens is a kind of porridge made by boiling water in which seeds of oats have been steeped for several days.

The Auld Farmer's New-Year-Morning Salutation to His Auld Mare, Maggie (p. 66). In the Kilmarnock MS, this poem follows *Address to the Deil*, which is mentioned in a letter of 17 February 1786; the likeliest date of composition, therefore, is early 1786. Burns glosses *The Auld Farmer's Salutation* with particular care in the Kilmarnock edition, noting the precise meaning of words as used by farmers in Ayrshire. His aim in the poem, written in the 'Standart Habby' stanza, is to convey the nature of the long and close relationship between farmer and favourite mare. He does this with realism, humour and tenderness. Avoiding excessive sentimentality, he suggests that they have grown old together naturally and with grace. The poem is addressed to Maggie throughout, but – with characteristic country humour – there is a hint that the farmer has affectionately identified together in his mind since his wedding-day (l. 32) Maggie the wedding-gift with his bride Jenny. Jenny has no doubt had to work just as hard as the loyal mare which once belonged to her father.

Title: A 'hansel' is a gift to mark a new beginning or special occasion, particularly a New Year gift.

21. *o' tocher clear*: Clear of, i.e. quite apart from, dowry.

35. KYLE-STEWART: the northern part of Kyle, Burns's district of Ayrshire, between the rivers Ayr and Irvine.

37. *hoyte*: 'the motion between a trot and gallop' (B).

51. *Brooses*: races at country-weddings, between the bridegroom's home and the bride's home or church.

57. *Scotch mile*: longer than the standard English mile by some 200 metres.

61. *Fittie-lan'*: The 'fit-o'-land' or left horse of the back pair in the plough team of four, which trod unploughed land while its partner walked in the furrow.

71. Till sprittie knowes . . . : Until rushy hillocks would have roared and torn away easily. An example of apt rural Scots which may have given difficulty even in 1786.

79. *car*: A kind of 'sledge', without wheels, made of two long birch or hazel branches, with wicker cross-pieces. The front ends were tied as shafts to the horse's collar while the rear ends were on the ground.

100. fow: A firlot, equivalent to almost one bushel of wheat or two bushels of barley and oats. Also used in the sense of a 'mow', that which has been forked.

106. To some hain'd rig . . . : The last three lines replace the MS reading:
   An' clap thy back,
  An' mind the days we've haen the gither,
   An' ca' the crack.

The Cotter's Saturday Night (p. 70). Written in the winter of 1785–6 – the setting is November (l. 10) – and mentioned by Burns as complete in his letter to Richmond of 17 February 1786. The father of the household in the poem is modelled at least in part on Burns's own father, William Burnes, who had died in 1784, worn out by toil on poor land. His piety and concern for his children's education led him to compile *A Manual of Religious Belief in a Dialogue between Father and Son*. Burns's brother Gilbert, who shared the same upbringing as the poet, comments on the central action in the poem, 'Robert had frequently remarked to me that he thought that there was something peculiarly venerable in the phrase, "Let us worship God", used by a decent sober head of a family introducing family worship (l. 108). To this sentiment . . . the world is indebted for *The Cotter's Saturday Night*.'

  Burns had a model for a naturalistic word-picture of a domestic farm scene in Fergusson's 'The Farmer's Ingle', written like his own poem in Spenserian stanzas. In a number of ways, however, 'The Cotter's Saturday Night' differs sharply from Fergusson's poem. Whereas 'The Farmer's Ingle' is wholly in Lowland Scots, Burns combines the vernacular with extended passages in English. This is because he is concerned to show the nature of the religious outlook and moral values of those he describes, while Fergusson's aim is genre description *per se*. The accepted language for religious and moral reflection in poetry in 18th-century Lowland Scotland was not Scots but English, which had been used in Bible and worship since the time of the Scottish Reformation. Again in contrast to Fergusson, who does not identify any love-interest among the members of his farming family, Burns with the story of Jenny and her wooer introduces a narrative episode centring on romantic love. This helps to broaden his poem's appeal. He has been heavily criticized by a number of 20th-century critics for the rather strained note he strikes in stanza 10 ('Is there, in human-form, that bears a heart – . . .'). But the communicative power of the whole poem is not in doubt. In its ambitious scope and tonal range 'The Cotter's Saturday Night' goes beyond Fergusson's reach in 'The Farmer's Ingle'.

Dedication: R. A****: Robert Aiken (1739–1807), solicitor and surveyor of taxes in Ayr, eldest son of an Ayr shipbuilder, and grandson of James Dalrymple, sheriff-clerk of Ayrshire. He met Burns *c.* 1783, and became a trusted friend and enthusiastic admirer of Burns's poems. He was a talented public speaker and reader of poetry; Burns commented that 'he read me into fame'. Aiken collected the names of 145 subscribers for the Kilmarnock edition.

10. November chill: Burns owes something to the opening of Fergusson's poem 'The Farmer's Ingle':

>Whan gloming grey out o'er the welkin keeks,
> Whan *Batie* ca's his owsen to the byre,
>Whan *Thrasher John*, sair dung, his barn-door steeks,
> And lusty lasses at the dighting tire . . .

but he also has in mind Gray's *Elegy*, ll. 2–3:

>The lowing herd wind slowly o'er the lea,
>The ploughman homeward plods his weary way.

13. black'ning trains: Thomson describes 'a blackening train of clamorous rooks' in 'Winter', ll. 140–1.

21ff. The expectant *wee-things*: Burns's original Scots rendering of a domestic scene which recurs in 18th-century poetry, with its ultimate source in Virgil's *Georgics*, Book II. cf. Gray's 'Elegy', ll. 21–4.

22. flichterin: Glossed by Burns in 1787 as 'to flutter as young nestlings when their dam approaches'.

23. His wee-bit ingle: cf. Ramsay, *The Gentle Shepherd*, I, ii, 179–80:

>In Winter, when he toils thro' Wind and Rain,
>A bleezing Ingle, and a clean Hearth-stane.

26. kiaugh and care: Revised in 1793 to 'carking cares', possibly because 'kiaugh' seemed obscure.

48. wi' an eydent hand: cf. 'The Farmer's Ingle', l. 29, 'to labouring lend an eidant hand'.

50. 'fear the LORD alway!': Burns recalls such texts as Psalm 34:9.

73. O happy love!: Burns writes in his first Commonplace Book, April 1783: 'If anything on earth deserves the name of rapture or transport it is the feelings of green eighteen in the company of the mistress of his heart when she repays him with an equal return of affection.'

82ff. Is there, in human form . . . : A modern critic has described this stanza as 'one of the most nauseating ever published by a reputable poet' (T. Crawford, *Burns: A Study of the Poems and Songs*, 1960, p. 179); but the poet's moral reflections held strong appeal for his contemporaries. James Kinsley accurately comments that the passage is 'an eighteenth-century set piece' (*The Poems and Songs of Robert Burns*, Oxford, 1968, p. 1115).

93. *Hawkie*: Cow with the white face, pet name.

96. weel-hain'd kebbuck: 'If cheese was to be kept for some time . . . all the whey had to be squeezed out, and pressing was a necessity . . . Ayrshire or Dunlop cheese became the country's national cheese.' (A. Fenton, *Scottish Country Life*, 1976, pp. 152, 154.)

111–14. *Dundee . . . Martyrs . . . Elgin*: Old psalm tunes, the first two being included in the Twelve 'Common Tunes' in the Scottish psalter of 1615, and 'Elgin' in the Scottish Psalter of 1625.

115. *Italian trills are tame*: Burns agrees with Fergusson ('Elegy on the Death of Scots Music', ll. 49–54) in deploring the fashionable preference for elaborate Italian musical performance over native Scottish 'simplicity'. cf. also William Hamilton of Bangour, who describes in Ode IV (*Poems on Several Occasions*, 1760) how cottagers

> Had, at the sober-tasted meal,
> Repeated oft, the grateful tale;
> Had hymn'd, in native language free,
> The song of thanks to heaven and thee;
> A music that the great ne'er hear,
> Yet sweeter to th'internal ear,
> Than any soft seducing note
> E'er thrill'd from Farinelli's throat.

117. Nae unison hae they: The Scottish tradition in psalmody was for everyone to keep the same pitch and sing together, in unison.

119. How *Abram*: cf. Genesis 12:1–2.

120–1. *Moses . . . Amalek*: cf. Exodus 17:9, 16.

122. the *royal Bard* did groaning lye: cf. Samuel 12:10–11, and Psalm 6.

130. Had not . . . whereon to lay His head: cf. Matthew 8:20, Luke 9:58.

131–2. How . . . to many a land: Burns recalls Acts and the New Testament epistles.

133. *he*, who lone in *Patmos*: cf. Revelation 1:8, 19:17.

135. *Bab'lon's* doom: cf. Revelation 18:10.

138. springs exulting: *Windsor Forest*, ll. 111–12.

141. No more . . . the bitter tear: cf. Isaiah 25:8; Revelation 7:17.

142. hymning their CREATOR'S praise: cf. *Paradise Lost*, vii, 258–9: '. . . hymning prais'd God and his Works, Creatour him they sung.'

153. *Book of Life*: cf. Revelation 3:5, 13:8.
158. HE who stills the *raven's* clam'rous nest: cf. Job 38:41, 'Who provideth for the raven his food? when his young ones cry unto God . . .'
159. And decks the *lily* fair: cf. Matthew 6:28, 'Consider the lilies of the field . . .'
163. From scenes like these: Burns echoes Thomson, 'Summer', ll. 423–4:

> A simple scene! yet hence Britannia sees
> Her solid grandeur rise.

165. Princes and lords: cf. Goldsmith, *The Deserted Village*, ll. 53–5:

> Princes and lords may flourish, or may fade;
> A breath can make them, as a breath has made:
> But a bold peasantry . . .

166. An honest man . . . : An echo of Pope, *Essay on Man*, iv, 248.
168. The *Cottage* leaves the *Palace*: Perhaps suggested by Fergusson's 'Retirement', ll. 45–8:

> In yonder lowly cot delight to dwell,
> And leave the statesman for the labouring hind,
> The regal palace for the lowly cell.

172. O SCOTIA!: Fergusson had written in 'The Farmer's Ingle', ll. 113–17:

> May SCOTIA'S simmers ay look gay and green,
>   Her yellow har'sts frae scowry blasts decreed;
> May a' her tenants sit fu' snug and bien,
>   Frae the hard grip of ails and poortith freed,
>   And a lang lasting train o' peaceful hours succeed.

181. the *patriotic tide*: William Wallace, victor of Stirling Bridge, was executed by Edward I of England in 1305. 'The story of Wallace poured a Scottish prejudice in my veins which will boil along there till the flood-gates of life shut in eternal rest' (*Letters* I. 136).
188. the *Patriot*, and the *Patriot-Bard*: cf. Coila's speech to the poet in 'The Vision', l. 109ff.

To a Mouse (p. 77). Dated by the poet November 1785. Burns's brother Gilbert stated that the 'verses to the *Mouse* and *Mountain-daisy*' were composed . . . 'while the author was holding the plough'. John Blane, who worked with Burns as gaudsman (driving the horses in front of the plough), commented many years after the event that he, being only a lad, had actually started to run after the mouse with the intention of killing it, when he was checked by Burns; the latter then became 'thoughtful and abstracted'. Whatever the degree of accuracy of Blane's recollection, *To a Mouse* conveys very directly Burns's tender concern for a defenceless creature. Drawing aptly and unobtrusively on the Bible, and also on the poet's reading of Johnson's *Rasselas*, it wryly underlines two ideas – the unity of creation, and the vulnerability of human beings as well as of small animals.

6. pattle: A small long-handled spade carried on a plough to clear it of mud, a plough-staff.

7–8. Man's dominion . . . Nature's social union: The idea of man as tyrant over the rest of creation is common in 18th-century poetry. cf. Pope, *Essay on Man*, iii, 147–64, and Thomson's *Seasons, passim*, e.g. 'Spring', ll. 702–5.

15. *daimen-icker*: Ayrshire Scots, denoting an occasional ear of corn. thrave: two stooks of corn, or 24 sheaves, a measure of straw or fodder.

17. I'll get a blessin wi' the lave: cf. 'When thou cuttest down thine harvest in thy field, and hast forgot a sheaf in the field, thou shalt not go again to fetch it: it shall be for the stranger, for the fatherless, and for the widow: that the Lord thy God may bless thee in all the work of thine hands' (Deuteronomy 24:19).

22. foggage: 'rank grass which has not been eaten in summer, or which grows among grain, and is fed on by horses and cattle after the crop is removed' (*Jamieson's Scots Dictionary*).

43–8. Still, thou art blest, compar'd wi' me!: cf. Johnson, *Rasselas*, chapter 2, 'As he passed through the fields, and saw the animals around him, "Ye," said he, "are happy, and need not envy me that walk thus among you, burdened with myself; nor do I, ye gentle beings, envy your felicity, for it is not the felicity of man. I have many distresses from which ye are free; I fear pain when I do not feel it; I sometimes shrink at evils recollected, and sometimes start at evils anticipated: surely the equity of Providence has balanced peculiar sufferings with peculiar enjoyments.'

Epistle to Davie (p. 78). Burns dates the finished poem January 1785, but part of it was drafted the previous year, probably before the idea of its inclusion in a verse epistle had occurred to him. His brother Gilbert commented, 'It was, I think, in the summer of 1784, when in the intervals of harder labour Robert and I were weeding in the garden, that he repeated to me the principal part of the *Epistle*.' By 'the principal part', Gilbert seems to have had in mind 'the poet pointing out the consolations that were in store for him when he should go a-begging', i.e. stanzas 2 to 7 or a sequence within them. The introductory and concluding stanzas, including the tribute to Jean Armour (l. 108ff.), were written later.

A tenant farmer's son, like Burns, David Sillar (1760–1830) was at this time a grocer in Irvine. He was a keen fiddler, as well as a poet; a manuscript of this poem is entitled 'An Epistle to Davy, a brother Poet, Lover, Ploughman and Fiddler'. A point of particular interest in the poem is that ll. 53–4,

> We'll sit and *sowth* a tune;
>
> Syne *rhyme* till't . . .

were to be fulfilled when Sillar's original tune 'A Rosebud' was used by Burns for his song 'A Rosebud by My Early Walk', first published in volume ii of *The Scots Musical Museum* (1788). Burns wrote a second Epistle to Davie before the Kilmarnock *Poems* were published. Sillar's own *Poems* appeared at Kilmarnock in 1789.

The 14-line stanza Burns uses here had been employed, as he himself noted, in Alexander Montgomerie's poem 'The Cherrie and the Slae', which he knew from Ramsay's anthology, *The Ever Green*. Ramsay himself had handled this complicated verse form in such poems as 'The Poet's Wish: An Ode', and Burns builds on Ramsay's example, seeking to link in fluent unity sestet, quatrain, and 'wheel' (with its demanding internal rhymes in ll. 11 and 13). It is arguable that the form does not allow him to achieve a conversational tone to the same degree as 'Standart Habby'; but any slight air of strain is limited to the 'wheel' at the end of certain stanzas.

1. frae off BEN-LOMOND: The winds blow from the north. Ben Lomond is in the Trossachs, to the north-east of Loch Lomond. It can be seen on the horizon from various points in Ayrshire.

7. blaw in the drift: The sense is that snow is driven by the wind right into the fireside.

25. 'Mair spier na, nor fear na,': From Ramsay's 'The Poet's Wish', ll. 53–6:

> Mair speer na, and fear na,
>
> But set thy mind to rest,
>
> Aspire ay still high'r ay,
>
> And always hope the best.

29. kilns: cf. 'Halloween', l. 96 and note.

54. *sowth* a tune: cf. an entry in the poet's First Commonplace Book: '. . . these old Scottish airs are so nobly sentimental that when one would compose to them; to south the tune, as our Scotch phrase is, over and over, is the readiest way to catch the inspiration'.

56ff. It's no in titles . . . : cf. Fergusson, 'Against Repining at Fortune', l. 41ff:

> 'Tis not in richest mines of Indian gold,
>
> That man this jewel happiness can find,
>
> If his unfeeling breast, to *virtue* cold,
>
> Denies her entrance to his ruthless mind.

> Wealth, pomp and honor are but gaudy toys;
> Alas! how poor the pleasures they impart!
> *Virtue's* the sacred source of all the joys
> That claim a lasting mansion in the heart.

77–80. Alas! how aft . . . : 'Moral indignation has caused Burns to slip un-
consciously into the intonation of the Scottish Metrical Psalms' (T.
Crawford, *Burns: A Study of the Poems and Songs*, 1960, p. 88).

91, 97. wit: Here 'knowledge, insight, understanding'.

107. MEG: Margaret Orr, a servant at Stair House. According to local
tradition, Burns helped to bring the couple together.

108. my darling JEAN: Jean Armour, Burns's future wife.

130–2. Long since . . . for you: cf. Sterne, *A Sentimental Journey:* '. . . illus-
ions, which cheat expectation and sorrow of their weary moments! –
long – long since had ye number'd out my days, had I not trod so great
a part of them upon this enchanted ground'.

The Lament (p. 83). Written in the spring or summer of 1786 out of
Burns's distress over the attitude shown to him by Jean Armour and her
parents: the 'friend' of the title is a fiction. The first of a group of poems in
the collection all of which reflect in varying degrees either Burns's low spirits
specifically at this time ('The Lament', 'Despondency, an Ode', 'To a
Mountain-Daisy'), or more generally the melancholy side of his nature ex-
pressed for other reasons ('Man Was Made to Mourn', 'Winter, A Dirge', 'A
Prayer in the Prospect of Death', 'To Ruin'). Burns chooses English in these
poems as the accepted language in which to express moral sentiment. Inter-
estingly, A. L. Taylor has argued that the arrangement of poems in the
Kilmarnock edition 'reveals Burns as a creative editor, using his poems to
hint at a story as if they were a sequence of sonnets' (*Burns Chronicle*, 3rd
series, vol. xii, 1963.) Whatever importance should be attached to alleged
cryptic autobiography in the edition as a whole, there can be no doubt that
'The Lament' is a cry from the heart. Burns commented in 1787 in a letter to
Dr John Moore: ''Twas a shocking affair, which I cannot yet bear to recollect;
and had very nearly given [me] one or two of the principal qualifications for a
place among those who have lost the chart and mistake the reckoning of
Rationality' (*Letters*, I. 144). What took place was this. Jean Armour's preg-
nancy became known to her parents in March, causing her father to faint
from shock. In April he persuaded the Ayr lawyer Robert Aiken to cut out the
names of the couple from a document which Burns had given to Jean promis-
ing marriage or stating that it had taken place. The Armours had hopes that a
suitor in Paisley more acceptable to themselves than Burns might still marry
Jean, despite her pregnancy, and sent her to relatives in that town: this plan

came to nothing. Burns meanwhile ran into 'all kinds of dissipation and riot, Mason-meetings, drinking matches, and other mischief, to drive her out of my head, but all in vain'. James Armour applied for a warrant against Burns, and when his *Poems* came out, the poet was virtually in hiding. He escaped any action at law, but, like Jean, was summoned before the Kirk Session, guardians of sexual *mores*. (Twins were born to Jean on 3 September. The next summer she was pregnant by Burns again, and in the spring of 1788 became Mrs Burns.) Burns retained 'The Lament' in unchanged form in later editions of his *Poems*. The metre of this poem is 'ballat royal', rhyming *ababbcbc*, a favourite with medieval Scots poets and with King James VI, who wrote, 'For any heich and grave suiectis . . . use this kynde of verse, callit Ballit Royal.' Burns had come across examples of the form in Ramsay's *Ever Green*.

Epigraph: From John Home, *Douglas: A Tragedy*, 1757 (Home's *Works*, ed. Mackenzie, 1822, i, 307).

   54. Recollection's direful train: cf. Goldsmith, *The Deserted Village*, l. 81, 'Remembrance wakes with all her busy train'.

Despondency (p. 86). Probably written like the preceding poem primarily to express Burns's hurt feelings over the Armour affair (see especially stanza 4). The stanza is that of Alexander Montgomerie's poem 'The Cherrie and the Slae', a combination of sestet, quatrain, and 'wheel'. cf. 'Epistle to Davie', where it is used for a quite different poetic purpose.

  7–10. Dim-backward . . . fear: Burns possibly has in mind *Rasselas*, chapter 2. cf. note on 'To a Mouse', ll. 39–40.

    22. Unfitted with an *aim*: cf. Burns to Moore, 'The great misfortune of my life was, never to have AN AIM' (letter of August 1787).

  31ff. Within his humble cell . . . : 18th-century literature contains many passages praising a retired country life. cf. here Parnell, 'The Hermit', ll. 3–4:

> The moss his bed, the cave his humble cell,
> His food the fruits, his drink the crystal well.

cf. also Fielding, *Tom Jones*, Book viii, chapter 15, 'a curious Discourse between Mr Jones and the Man of the Hill'.

Man Was Made to Mourn (p. 88). Copied into the poet's first Commonplace Book in August 1785. There Burns names as the tune for his 'song' the Irish air 'Peggy Bawn'. A letter to Mrs Dunlop of 16 August 1788 shows how strongly Burns felt on this subject: 'Man is by no means a happy creature. – I do not speak of the Selected Few, favored by partial Heaven . . . I speak of the neglected Many, whose nerves, whose sinews, whose days, whose thoughts . . . are sacrificed and sold to these few bloated Minions of Heaven! – if I thought you had never seen it, I would transcribe you a stanza of an old Scots Ballad called "The life and ages of Man" . . . I had an old Grand uncle, with whom my Mother lived a while in her girlish years . . . long blind ere he died . . . his most voluptuous enjoyment was to sit down and cry, while my Mother would sing the simple old song.' The poet's brother Gilbert comments that, 'Burns could not well conceive a more mortifying picture of human life, than a man seeking work. In casting about in his mind how this sentiment might be brought forward, the elegy *Man was made to Mourn*, was composed.'

Tune, 'Peggy Bawn':

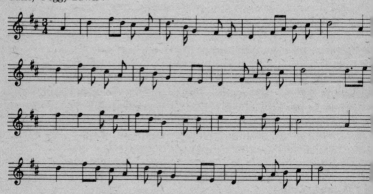

5. I spy'd a man, whose aged step: Like the 'hermit' mentioned in the previous poem, the elderly sage who meets and gives advice to a younger man is a common figure in 18th-century poetry. cf. Coleridge's ancient mariner, and Wordsworth's leech-gatherer.

17. yon moors: The manuscript reading 'Carrick Moors' shows that Burns originally had in mind the estate of the Earl of Cassillis.

34. Manhood's active might: Burns borrows this phrase from Shenstone, *Elegies*, xi, stanza 12.

55. Man's inhumanity to Man: cf. Edward Young, *Night Thoughts*, viii, 104–5, 'Man's . . . endless inhumanities on Man'.

60. To give him leave to toil: De Quincey refers to 'those groans which ascended to heaven from [Burns's] over-burthened heart – those harrowing words, "To give him leave to toil", which record almost a reproach to the ordinances of God' (*Collected Writings of Thomas De Quincey*, ed. Masson, Edinburgh, 1899, ii, p. 137).

Winter (p. 91). 'The eldest of my printed pieces' (Burns to Dr Moore, August 1787). In his first Commonplace Book, the title is 'Song – (Tune McPherson's Farewell)', and the entry is dated April 1784. There Burns comments, 'As I am, what the men of the world, if they knew of such a man would call a whimsical Mortal; I have various sources of pleasure & enjoyment which are, in a manner, peculiar to myself; or some here & there such other out-of-the-way person. – Such is the peculiar pleasure I take in the season of Winter, more than the rest of the year – This, I believe, may be partly owing to my misfortunes giving my mind a melancholy cast; but there is something even in the –

> "–Mighty tempest & the hoary waste
>   Abrupt & deep stretch'd o'er the buried earth–"

which raises the mind to a serious sublimity, favorable to every thing great & noble. – There is scarcely any earthly object gives me more – I don't know if I should call it pleasure, but something which exalts me, something which enraptures me – than to walk in the sheltered side of a wood or high plantation, in a cloudy, winter day, and hear a stormy wind howling among the trees & raving o'er the plain. – It is my best season for devotion; – my mind is rapt up in a kind of enthusiasm to Him who, in the pompous language of Scripture, "walks on the winds of the wind". – In one of these seasons, just after a tract of misfortunes, I composed the following SONG – (Tune McPherson's Farewell).' 'Winter' may have been written in 1781–2.

In responding positively to the severe beauty of winter (cf. 'In . . . the hoary majesty of WINTER, the poet feels a charm unknown to the rest of his species', letter to Margaret Kennedy, autumn 1785), Burns is at one with earlier Scottish poets, including James Thomson, whose poem *The Seasons* he knew and admired.

Tune, 'McPherson's Farewell':

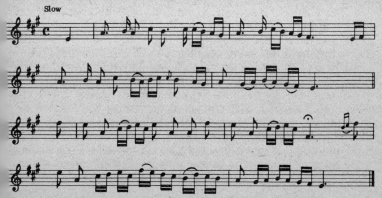

A Prayer, in the Prospect of Death (p. 92). An entry in the first Commonplace Book, dated August 1784, describes this as 'A prayer, when fainting fits, & other alarming symptoms of a Pleurisy or some other dangerous disorder, which indeed still threaten me, first put Nature on the alarm'. The poem may have been written much earlier than August 1784. Burns wrote to his father from Irvine on 27 December 1781, 'The weakness of my nerves has so debilitated my mind that I dare not, either review past events, or look forward into futurity . . . I am quite transported at the thought that ere long, perhaps very soon, I shall bid an eternal adiew to all the pains, & uneasiness & disquietudes of this weary life.' While the poet has in mind Pope's *Universal Prayer*, which is more than once echoed in his poem, his metre is that of the Scottish metrical psalms.

To a Mountain-Daisy (p. 93). Written in April 1786, during Burns's trouble with Jean Armour's family. He wrote to John Kennedy from Mossgiel on 20 April, '. . . I have here, likewise, inclosed a small piece, the very latest of my productions. I am a good deal pleas'd with some sentiments myself, as they are just the native querulous feelings of a heart, which, as the elegantly melting Gray says, "Melancholy has marked for her own".' (Kennedy, 1757–1812, was factor to the Earl of Dumfries, and later to the Earl of Breadalbane; he received copies of several of Burns's poems in manuscript and was active in securing subscriptions for the Kilmarnock edition.) *To a Mountain-Daisy* won the praise of early reviewers, Henry Mackenzie drawing attention to it as an example of 'the tender and the moral'. Recent critics, however, have tended to prefer *To a Mouse* – on which, to some degree, the later poem is modelled – as being stronger in diction and less strained in sentiment than *To a Mountain-Daisy*.

To Ruin (p. 95). Undated, but probably belonging to Burns's unhappy period learning flax-dressing in Irvine in 1781–2. 'My Partner was a scoundrel of the first water who made money by the mystery of thieving . . . I was oblidged to give up business; the clouds of misfortune were gathering thick round my father's head, the darkest of which was, he was visibly far gone in a consumption; and to crown all, a belle–fille whom I adored and who had pledged her soul to me in the field of matrimony, jilted me with peculiar circumstances of mortification [cf. ll.9–10]. – The finishing evil that brought up the rear of this infernal file was my hypochondriac complaint being irritated to such a degree, that for three months I was in [a] diseased state of body and mind' (letter to Dr John Moore, August 1787). The stanza is that of 'Epistle to Davie' and of 'Despondency, an Ode'.

Epistle to a Young Friend (p. 96). Dated in the MS at Kilmarnock 15 May 1786. The 'young friend' of the title was Ayr lawyer Robert Aiken's son Andrew, subsequently a merchant in Liverpool and British consul in Riga. (After Burns's death, William Niven of Kirkoswald claimed that the poem was originally addressed to him. He had, however, kept no copy to make good his case.)

The double stanza, with feminine rhyme, was familiar to Burns from the example of Ramsay.

In preparing the poem for publication, Burns reversed the order of stanzas 3 and 4, and omitted a MS stanza after 6:

> If ye hae made a step aside,
>> Some hap-mistake, o'ertaen you;
> Yet, still keep up a decent pride,
>> An' ne'er owre far demean you.
> Time comes wi' kind, oblivious shade,
>> An' daily darker sets it;
> An', if nae mae mistakes are made,
>> The world soon forgets it.

15. views: Plans, purposes.

87–8. may ye better reck the *rede*: cf. *Hamlet*, I, iii, 47–51:

> Doe not as some ungracious Pastors doe,
> Shew me the steepe and thorny way to Heaven;
> Whilst like a puft and recklesse Libertine
> Himselfe, the Primrose path of dalliance treads,
> And reaks not his own reade.

On a Scotch Bard Gone to the West Indies (p. 99). Written when Burns had decided to emigrate. His earliest reference to the idea is in a letter of *c.* 20 April 1786 to John Arnot: 'Already the holy beagles, the houghmagandie pack [fornication pack, i.e. the kirk session], begin to snuff the scent, & I expect every moment to see them cast off, & hear them after me in full cry [because of Jean Armour's pregnancy]: but as I am an old fox, I shall give them dodging and doubling for it; &, by & bye, I intend to earth among the mountains of Jamaica' (*Letters* I. 37). The position Burns had in view was that of book-keeper on a plantation at Port Antonio. By the time of publication of his *Poems*, he had 'orders within three weeks at farthest to repair aboard the Nancy, Captn Smith, from Clyde, to Jamaica, and to call at Antigua' (to John Richmond, 30 July 1786). The date of sailing was put off from week to week, however, and by early October 'the feelings of a father' prevented Burns from emigrating (letter to Robert Aiken, *c.* 8 October). He did not entirely give up the idea even then, writing to James Smith as late as June 1787 'if I do not fix, I will go for Jamaica'.

Turning on a theme which to most people would not immediately suggest humour, 'On a Scotch Bard Gone to the West Indies' is nevertheless a defiantly playful poem, a fluent and full-blooded exercise in Scots comic elegy. On the stanza, see introductory note on 'Poor Mailie's Elegy', p. 143.

20ff. Hadst thou taen aff some drowsy bummle: Burns boasts about his own sexual prowess ('gleg as onie wumble'), contrasted with 'some drowsy' bungler.

25. KYLE may weepers wear: Burns's native district of Ayrshire. 'Weepers' were thin stripes of linen worn on the cuffs to denote mourning.

33. A Jillet: Jean Armour.

56. Your native soil was right ill-willie: Burns has in mind his own Ayrshire parish, and long experience of uneconomic farms.

A Dedication To G**** H******* Esq (p. 101). In a verse epistle to Hamilton dated 3 May 1786, Burns writes

> The PRAY'R still, you share still,
>
>   Of grateful MINSTREL BURNS.

This reference to what appears here between ll. 90 and 112 of the 'Dedication' shows that at least one part of it, if not the entire poem, was drafted before 3 May. One argument in favour of such a date for the whole poem is that Burns's *Proposals* for publishing his work were in print by 15 April; it is known that Gavin Hamilton was active in distributing copies. It is possible, however, that the 'Dedication' as a whole belongs to May or even June – Burns may have worked his 'prayer' for Hamilton and his family into a new poetic context for the occasion. The poems went to the printer in mid-June. Hans Hecht was probably right to argue that Burns's original intention was to end the Kilmarnock collection with the 'Dedication'; he added a further group of poems on finding that he had not enough copy to make up the book to the length envisaged (Hecht, *Robert Burns*, 1936, p.95).

Gavin Hamilton (1751–1805), who sublet Mossgiel to Burns and his brother Gilbert in 1784, was a 'writer' (solicitor), living in Beechgrove, the so-called 'Castle of Mauchline', next to the village churchyard. He came of an Episcopalian family, and he himself sympathized with the Moderate rather than with the 'Auld Licht', tightly orthodox, wing of the Church of Scotland. These were two of the factors behind a long and bitter wrangle between Mauchline Kirk Session and Hamilton, which resulted in Hamilton's appealing over the heads of the Session to the Presbytery of Ayr and thus being granted by the Session in July 1785 a certificate that he was 'free from public scandal or ground of Church censure' known to them. Burns, who rejoiced in Hamilton's refusal to yield during this affair, wrote one of his most biting satires, 'Holy Willie's Prayer', to mark the discomfiture of Willie Fisher, an elder who had been particularly hostile to Hamilton. (The Session did not give up easily, prosecuting Hamilton for causing his servants to dig new potatoes in his garden on the 'last Lord's day' of July 1787.)

As in 'The Twa Dogs', Burns uses the octosyllabic couplet. His original plan may have been to open and close the collection with poems using this metre.

5. sirnam'd like *His Grace*: When questioned by the Duke of Hamilton about their relationship, Gavin Hamilton's father John is said to have replied that 'it would be needless to seek the root among the branches'.

28. He downa see a poor man want: Burns is at pains to make clear that Hamilton is generous to those in need because Mauchline Kirk Session had accused Hamilton of fraudulently retaining money collected for the parish poor.

42. *Gentoos*: Pagan Hindus, in contrast to Moslems (from Portuguese *gentio*, 'gentile').

43. *Ponotaxi*: Probably Cotopaxi, a volcano in the Andes.

48. This line was dropped from subsequent editions.

57–77. O ye wha leave the springs o' C-lv-n: Hugh Blair advised Burns to omit this paragraph from his 1787 Edinburgh *Poems*: 'The Poem will be much better without it, and it will give offence by the ludicrous views of the punishments of Hell.' Burns did not act on his advice.

77–80. digression . . . Divinity: See introductory note.

97. the CLERK: Hamilton was clerk of local courts.

100. K******'s: Hamilton's wife was Helen Kennedy of Daljarrock.

102. at least a diz'n: Hamilton had in fact two daughters, and two sons.

To a Louse (p. 105). Probably written in late 1785. That year saw several balloon flights over Scotland by the Italian Vincenzo Lunardi, who gave his name to a balloon-shaped bonnet (l. 35): the gently satirical poem is up-to-date in its reference to fashion. In 18th-century Scotland the louse was a common sight. Burns enjoys the idea that this particular louse evidently does not know its place; it is no respecter of Jenny's airs and graces. The success of the poem comes from Burns's mastery of the 'Standart Habby' verse form. He creates, and manages to sustain, a familiar conversational tone, almost a church whisper, by turns 'shocked' and amused, to match the cheeky movement of the louse on the unsuspecting girl's showy bonnet; and incidentally comments on the congregation's response to Jenny:

> Thae *winks* and *finger-ends*, I dread,
>   Are notice takin!

Burns's intimate way of speaking to the louse, as to a naughty child, is reminiscent of the technique used in 'Address to the Deil'.

Epistle to J. L***k** (p. 107). John Lapraik (1727–1807) was a tenant-farmer who had fallen on hard times: in 1785 he was imprisoned for debt in Ayr. While in prison, he wrote poetry for diversion. Following Burns's example, he published *Poems on Several Occasions* at Kilmarnock in 1788. His last years were spent as postmaster and innkeeper in Muirkirk.

Burns's first epistle to Lapraik shows him taking the initiative in contacting a stranger, a fellow-poet of the district, and defining his own characteristic priorities as a writer. The opening describes a 'rocking', a particular kind of social evening when songs and stories were to the fore. Burns responds to the personal (husband to wife) motif in the song by Lapraik which he hears sung. (Years later, he was to send a version of Lapraik's song to James Johnson for inclusion in *The Scots Musical Museum*.) He then goes on to project an image of himself as a spontaneous and instinctive 'rhymer', with no need for academic or critical pretensions ('Gie me ae spark o' Nature's fire . . .', ll. 73–8). His hope is to catch a spark of the inspiration which burns in Allan Ramsay and Fergusson. Reaffirming his wish to meet Lapraik as a friend and 'hae a swap o' *rhyming-ware*', he strongly rejects by contrast the values of people whose efforts are directed towards money-making.

7. a rockin: The Rev. John Sheppard of Muirkirk described a rocking as taking place 'when neighbours visit one another in pairs, or three or more in company, during the moonlight of winter or spring . . . The custom seems to have arisen when spinning on the *rock* or *distaff* was in use, which therefore was carried along with the visitant to a neighbour's house, [and] still prevails, though the *rock* is laid aside' (*Memories of Ayrshire about 1780*, ed. W. Kirk Dickson, Scottish History Society, Miscellany vi, 1939, p. 288).

13. ae *sang*: 'When I upon thy bosom lean', said to have been written when Lapraik's wife had been fretting over their misfortunes. Lapraik included the song in his *Poems on Several Occasions* (Kilmarnock, 1788), and Burns supplied an improved version in Scots for *The Scots Musical Museum* (no. 205, 1780).

21–2. *Pope . . . Steele . . . Beattie*: Here as examples of writers skilled in expressing moral sentiments. Burns was familiar with the poetry of Pope, and with Steele's periodical essays. James Beattie (1735–1803), professor of moral philosophy at Aberdeen, was best known for his blank verse poem, *The Minstrel*, although he also wrote Scots verse.

24. About *Muirkirk*: Lapraik lived at Dalfram, on Ayr Water, about nine miles from Mauchline, and near the village of Muirkirk.

28–30. The version of these lines in the first Commonplace Book reads:

> He was a devil
> But had a frank & friendly heart
> Discreet & civil.

45. *crambo-jingle*: cf. Hamilton of Gilbertfield, Epistle 1 to Allan Ramsay, ll. 49–50:

> At Crambo then we'll rack our Brain,
> Drown ilk dull Care and aiking Pain.

61f. What's a your jargon: cf. Pomfret, *Reason* (1700), ll. 57–8:

> What's all the noisy jargon of the schools
> But idle nonsense of laborious fools . . .

73. Gie me ae Spark: cf. Sterne, *Tristram Shandy*, III, xii, 'Great Apollo! if thou art in a giving humour – give me – I ask no more, but one stroke of native humour, with a single spark of thy own fire along with it.'

79. ALLAN: Allan Ramsay.

80. FERGUSSON: Robert Fergusson. 'Rhyme, except some religious pieces, which are in print, I had given up; but meeting with Fergusson's Scotch Poems, I strung anew my wildly-sounding, rustic lyre with emulating vigour' (letter to John Moore, August 1787).

103. MAUCHLINE Race or MAUCHLINE Fair: In suggesting a convivial meeting between poets, Burns follows the example of Hamilton of Gilbertfield in his first Epistle to Ramsay. Hamilton writes, 'At Edinburgh we'll hae a Bottle of reaming claret' (l.45).

To the Same (p. 111). Burns follows up in his second epistle to Lapraik by condemning mere materialistic or snobbish values and once again asserting the strong claims of poetry and human fellowship:

> The social, friendly, honest man . . .
> 'Tis *he* fulfils *great Nature's plan*,
> And none but *he*.

Two points of particular interest in this poem are the admission – in April 1785, when he was particularly prolific – that his Muse had recently been very busy (ll. 15–16), and the emphasis on writing as a form of improvisation:

> Sae I've begun to scrawl, but whether
> In rhyme, or prose, or baith thegither . . .
> Let time mak proof.

1. new-ca'd kye: Burns is probably recalling a line of Ramsay's, 'And late calf'd Cows stand lowing near their Home' (*Works*, STS, i, 111).

6. kind *letter*: Lapraik's reply, now lost, was in prose, not verse.

8. Rattlin the corn: Burns describes spring sowing.

19. Her dowf excuses pat me mad: c.f. the teasing relationship between poet and Muse in Ramsay's 'Answer II' to Hamilton of Gilbertfield, l. 25ff.

49. She's gien me monie a jirt an' fleg: The image comes from ploughing, as Burns recalls jolting moments in his life, when he has met hidden 'stones'.

69. nae *sheep-shank bane:* The sense is 'no small beer'.

87. The social . . . man: cf. Pope, *Essay on Man*, iv, 341–60:

> God will favour and approve the man
> Who most observes and best pursues his plan:
> His plan, that ev'ry creature, ev'ry soul,
> Should spread the good which he designs the whole;
> To this, that action, passion, reason tend;
> VIRTUE the means, and HAPPINESS the end.

To W. S***** (p.114). William Simson (1758–1815), the son of a farmer at Ochiltree, five miles south of Burns's home at Mossgiel, studied at Glasgow University with a view to entering the ministry, but instead became schoolmaster at Ochiltree. According to tradition, he wrote to Burns to praise 'The Holy Tulzie', a hard-hitting church satire (not included in the Kilmarnock edition). Someone with his knowledge of the Church of Scotland was clearly in a good position to appreciate the postscript to this epistle, with its satire on the current ecclesiastical division between 'Auld Lichts' and 'New Lichts' as 'moonshine matter' (l. 182). Whether or not the postscript was added as an afterthought, Burns follows a sound instinct in keeping it separate from the main part of the poem, in which he expresses friendship and his delight in poetry and in nature, themes belonging to the main tradition of the verse epistle in 18th-century Scotland.

13. in a creel: Confused, in a whirl, lit. in a basket (full of stones). A 'creeling' took place on the second day after a wedding, as a means of showing whether the marriage had been consummated. A basket of stones being placed on the bridegroom's back, 'if he has acted a manly Part, his young Wife with all imaginable Speed cuts the Cords, and relieves him from the Burthen' (Ramsay, *Works*, STS, i, 78).

15. *Allan . . . Gilbertfield*: The Scottish poets Allan Ramsay and William Hamilton of Gilbertfield.

17. the writer-chiel: Robert Fergusson had worked as a copyist in the

Commissary Office in Edinburgh, for which he was paid a penny a page.

31. COILA: The Muse of Kyle, Burns's district of Ayrshire. cf. 'The Vision'.

40. *New Holland*: Australia. The Dutch had discovered the western coasts of the southern continent on their voyages round the Cape of Good Hope to the East Indies.

42. *Magellan*: In 1520 Ferdinand Magellan discovered the strait between South America and Tierra del Fuego.

44f. *Forth an' Tay*: cf. a passage in Burns's First Commonplace Book: 'we have never had one Scotch Poet of any eminence, to make the fertile banks of Irvine, the romantic woodlands & sequestered scenes on Aire, and the heathy, mountainous source, & winding sweep of Doon emulate Tay, Forth, Ettrick, Tweed &c this is a complaint I would gladly remedy'. In his poem 'Hame Content', ll. 75–82, Fergusson asks if the Arno and

> Tiber are 'mair sweet and gay
> Than Fortha's haughs or banks o' Tay'.

61. At WALLACE' name: William Wallace, Scottish patriot, executed by Edward I of England in 1305. Burns wrote to Moore, 'The two first books I ever read in private, and which gave me more pleasure than any two books I ever read again, were the life of Hannibal and the history of Sir William Wallace ... The story of Wallace poured a Scotish prejudice in my veins which will boil along there till the flood-gates of life shut in eternal rest' (August 1787, *Letters* I. 136).

73f. Ev'n winter bleak has charms ... cf. 'Winter, A Dirge' and introductory note; and Thomson, 'Autumn', ll. 1302–30:

> To Nature's voice attends from month to month,
> And day to day, through the revolving year –
> Admiring, sees her in her every shape; ...
> Even Winter wild to him is full of bliss.

88. An' no think lang: cf. Alexander Ross, 'The Fortunate Shepherd', ll. 731–2:

> While Henny's ay the burthen o' his sang,
> And ever keeps his mind frae thinking lang.

92. Hog-shouther: 'a kind of horse play by justling with the shoulder; to justle' (B).

103. While Highlandmen hate tolls an' taxes: One legacy of Culloden was that Hanoverian rule was resented. Despite problems of communication, Highlanders preferred the old drove roads of Scotland to expensive turnpike trusts.

104. braxies: Sheep that have died of 'the braxy', an internal infection.

Burns refers to a common belief among shepherds that eating braxy was not a health risk.

112. this *new-light*: William Taylor of Norwich argued in *The Scripture Doctrine of Original Sin proposed to free and candid Examination* (1740) that in interpreting scripture 'we ought not to admit anything contradictory to the common sense and understanding of mankind'. His book was widely accepted as summing up the 'New Light Rationalism'.

119. in plain, braid lallans: Burns's contemporary Henry Mackenzie noted that 'though our books be written in *English*, our conversation is in *Scotch* . . . we have a suit for holidays and another for working-days' (*The Mirror*, no. 83, 22 February 1780).

152. bure sic hands: Fought with such vigour.

170. things they ca' *balloons*: Balloon flights were making news in 1785. cf. 'To a Louse', introductory note.

Epistle to J. R****** (p. 120). Written probably late in 1784. The poem was occasioned by the pregnancy of Burns's serving-girl at Lochlea, Elizabeth Paton, who bore him a daughter on 22 May 1785. Burns recounts the episode in sporting metaphors, from love-making to the predictable reaction of the parish elders to an unmarried girl's pregnancy. This masculine humour no doubt appealed strongly to John Rankine (d.1810), a tenant farmer in Adamhill, Tarbolton, one of Burns's 'ramstam' cronies of the Lochlea years. Hugh Blair, Edinburgh professor and critic, was shocked by the poem, however. He advised against keeping it in the 1787 edition in these terms: 'The description of shooting the hen is understood, I find, to convey an indecent meaning, tho' in reading the poem . . . I took it literally, and the indecency did not strike me. But . . . the whole poem ought undoubtedly to be left out of the new edition.' Burns did not act on his advice, and the epistle remained in all editions of his poems published in his lifetime.

4. *dreams*: Burns's early 19th-century editor Allan Cunningham supplies details: 'Lord K— [who] was in the practice of calling all his familiar acquaintances . . . "damned brutes" was rebuked by Rankine, who said, 'I dreamed I was dead, and that for keeping other than good company on earth I was damned. When I knocked at hell-door . . . quoth Satan, "ye canna be here; ye're ane of Lord K—'s damned brutes – hell's fou o' them already!"'

5. Korah-like, a sinkin: Korah and his people did not 'die the common death of all men'. 'The earth opened her mouth, and swallowed them up, and their houses, and . . . all their goods' (Numbers 16:29–33).

20. *Blue-gown* badge: Like the badge and clothing of the King's bedes-men, licensed beggars in Scotland since the Middle Ages.

36. *Bunker's hill:* Sir William Howe gained a British victory at Bunker Hill in the American War of Independence.

47. *Poacher-Court:* The Kirk Session had power to require sexual trans-gressors to pay fines and to sit on the 'stool of repentance' before the congregation.

65. *buckskin* kye: American plantation slaves. 'Buckskin' was a nickname applied to American troops during the War of Indepen-dence. cf. Burns to Dr Moore, letter of August 1787, 'I resolved to publish my Poems . . . 'twas a delicious idea that I should be called a clever fellow, even tho' it should never reach my ears a poor Negro-driver.' (*Letters* I. 144).

75. *pennyworths* again is fair: Value for money.

Song, It was upon a Lammas night (p. 123). Burns stated that this song was written before his twenty-third year: the actual time of composi-tion is unrecorded. He was to note many years after 1786, 'All the old words that ever I could meet to this [air] were the following, which seem to have been an old chorus:-

> O corn rigs and rye rigs,
>> O corn rigs are bonie,
> And when'er you meet a bonnie lass,
>> Preen up her cockernony.

He also knew Ramsay's song 'My Patie Is a Lover Gay' from *The Gentle Shepherd*, which ends

> Then I'll comply and marry Pate,
>> And syne my cockernony
> He's free to touzle air and late
>> Where corn rigs are bony.

In performance, this is one of Burns's most successful love-songs, proving that he was able even at this early date to match his words to the spirit of a traditional tune. In comparison with Ramsay's song, 'It was upon a Lammas night' is thoroughly personal. Whereas Ramsay offers a conventional ex-ample of pastoral verse love-description, tinged with genteel eroticism, Burns writes in the first person and achieves a note of delight in remembered passion. The identity of Annie is not known, although the youngest daughter of John Rankine (see previous poem and introductory note) later claimed the honour. The tune probably originated in Scotland, although its 17th-century printings are English.

Tune, 'Corn rigs are bonie':

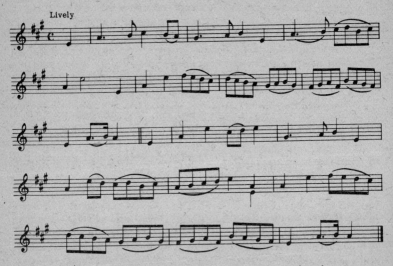

1. Lammas: 1 August, harvest festival when new bread was con-
   secrated. Here the sense is 'late summer', or more specifically
   'harvest night in August'.
2. rigs: Broad arable ridges which sloped towards ditches.
5. head: Burns changed this word to 'heed' in the 1793 edition. The
   phrase 'tentless heed' occurs in 'To J. S****', l. 55.

Song, 'Now westlin winds' (p. 124). Written in 1775 at the time of
Burns's infatuation with Peggy Thomson of Kirkoswald. 'I spent my
seventeenth summer,' he wrote in his autobiographical letter to Dr Moore in
August 1787, 'on a smuggling [coast] a good distance from home at a noted
school, to learn Mensuration, Surveying, Dialling, &c . . . I went on with a
high hand in my Geometry; till the sun entered Virgo, a month which is
always a carnival in my bosom, a charming Fillette who lived next door to
the school overset my Trigonomertry, and set me off in a tangent from the
sphere of my studies.' Later, he tried out a modification of this early song in
honour of Jean Armour; no known copy survives. Going back to the same
song, Burns then sent a version which has a number of Scots words in place of
the original English diction to be printed in *The Scots Musical Museum* (vol.
iv, 1792, no. 351). Unusually for a love-song, 'Now westlin winds' includes
four lines of protest against the 'slaught'ring guns' of sportsmen (ll. 21–4).

Tune, 'I had a horse, I had nae mair':

Very slow

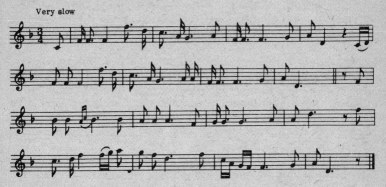

Song, 'From thee, Eliza' (p. 126). The first stanza suggests a date of composition shortly before the Kilmarnock *Poems* were published, and the position of the song in the collection immediately before 'The Farewell' also seems to point to the summer of 1786. If so, possibly 'Eliza' is Elizabeth Miller of Mauchline: in a letter to Smith dated 11 June 1787, Burns refers to 'my quondam Eliza'. However, any such identification is speculative, and it must be remembered that elsewhere Burns refers to this song as having been written before his twenty-third year (letter to Moore, August 1787). (It may be that the song existed in an early form before Burns wrote this version with its opening lines about having to leave his 'native shore'.)

Tune, 'Gilderoy':

Slow

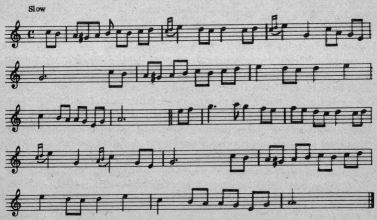

The Farewell (p. 126). Written in the early summer of 1786, possibly for a Masonic meeting on 24 June of St James's Lodge, Tarbolton, of which Burns had been depute master since July 1784. The song makes use throughout of the special language and terms of freemasonry, to which Burns was first introduced in 1781. (See William Harvey, 'Robert Burns as a Freemason', in *Robert Burns: Complete Works and Letters* [Masonic Edition], Glasgow [1928], v–xxxiv.) The tune to which 'The Farewell' is set was that of the then traditional Scottish parting-song (eventually to be replaced in public favour by Burns's highly popular song to the tune 'Auld Lang Syne'). Burns asked James Johnson to print 'The Farewell', with the accompanying air, as the final song in *The Scots Musical Museum*, and Johnson complied with his request (*SMM*, vol. vi, 1803, no. 600).

Tune, 'Goodnight and joy be wi' you a' ':

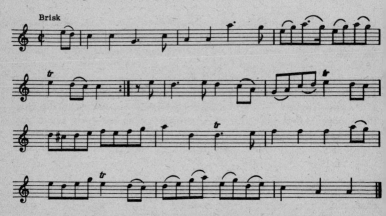

25. And YOU, farewell!: The master of the Lodge was Captain James Montgomerie, a younger brother of Colonel Hugh Montgomerie, afterwards Earl of Eglinton.

EPIGRAMS AND EPITAPHS (pp. 128–31).
Burns was a ready wit, with the ability to rhyme quickly and spontaneously. The brief selection of epigrams and epitaphs in the Kilmarnock edition is likely to have been included mainly to add to the length of the volume, although the poet must have felt more positively than this suggests about at least one epitaph, that 'For the Author's Father'.

Epitaph on a Henpecked Country Squire. A note in Burns's hand in a copy of the Kilmarnock *Poems* shows that 'Epitaph on a Henpecked Country Squire' and the two epigrams which follow it were written about Mr and Mrs William Campbell of Netherplace, a mansion near Mauchline. William Campbell died in 1786. The local talk was obviously unflattering to Campbell's widow, identified as Queen N[etherplace] in 'Another', l. 5.

On a Celebrated Ruling Elder. Dated April 1784 in the First Commonplace Book, where the subject is identified as 'Wm Hood, senr. in Tarbolton'.

On a Noisy Polemic. About James Humphrey, a mason in Mauchline. Burns uses 'polemic' in the sense 'argumentative person'. At this time 'bitch' (l. 3) was a term of contempt applied to either a man or a woman.

On Wee Johnie. Possibly about John Wilson, Tarbolton schoolmaster and apothecary, the object of Burns's satire in 'Death and Doctor Hornbook'; based on an English translation of a Latin epigram printed in *Nugae Venales*, 1663.

For the Author's Father. William Burnes died at Lochlea on 13 February 1784. This 'Epitaph on My Ever Honoured Father' is entered in the First Commonplace Book under April 1784. It is also engraved on the tombstone in Alloway Churchyard.

    8. 'For ev'n his failings lean'd to Virtue's side': The *Deserted Village*, l. 164.

For R. A. Esq. For Burns's 'lov'd . . . friend' Robert Aiken (see 'The Cotter's Saturday Night', l. 1, and note).

For G. H. Esq. For Gavin Hamilton. cf. 'A Dedication to G. H. Esq', and introductory note.

A Bard's Epitaph. Possibly written not long after the 'Epistle to a Young Friend', which is dated 15 May 1786. Burns describes himself as a man 'whose judgement clear, Can others teach the course to steer' (ll. 13–14).

    He wrote several poems in a wry confessional vein, showing self-knowledge and also the ability to laugh at himself. A well known example is the 'Elegy on the Death of Robert Ruisseaux', with its revealing final stanza:

Tho' he was bred to kintra wark,
And counted was baith wight and stark,
Yet that was never Robin's mark,
    To mak a man;
But tell him, he was learn'd and clark,
    Ye roos'd him then!

Though sombre in comparison, 'A Bard's Epitaph' is in its own way no less characteristic, recalling in its concluding lines the practical advice offered in the 'Epistle to a Young Friend'.

Appendix A

Burns's Preface and Glossary
in *Poems, Chiefly in the Scottish Dialect*
(Kilmarnock, 1786)

PREFACE

The following trifles are not the production of the Poet, who, with all the advantages of learned art, and perhaps amid the elegancies and idlenesses of upper life, looks down for a rural theme, with an eye to Theocrites or Virgil. To the Author of this, these and other celebrated names their countrymen are, in their original languages, 'A fountain shut up, and a 'book sealed'. Unacquainted with the necessary requisites for commencing Poet by rule, he sings the sentiments and manners, he felt and saw in himself and his rustic compeers around him, in his and their native language. Though a Rhymer from his earliest years, at least from the earliest impulses of the softer passions, it was not till very lately, that the applause, perhaps the partiality, of Friendship, wakened his vanity so far as to make him think any thing of his was worth showing; and none of the following works were ever composed with a view to the press. To amuse himself with the little creations of his own fancy, amid the toil and fatigues of a labouring life; to transcribe the various feelings, the loves, the griefs, the hopes, the fears, in his own breast; to find some kind of counterpoise to the struggles of a world, always an alien scene, a task uncouth to the poetical mind; these were his motives for courting the Muses, and in these he found Poetry to be its own reward.

Now that he appears in the public character of an Author, he does it with fear and trembling. So dear is fame to the rhyming tribe, that even he, an obscure, nameless Bard, shrinks aghast, at the thought of being branded as 'An impertinent blockhead, obtruding his nonsense on the world; and because he can make a shift to jingle a few doggerel, Scotch rhymes together, looks upon himself as a Poet of no small consequence forsooth'.

It is an observation of that celebrated Poet,* whose divine Elegies do honor to our language, our nation, and our species, that 'Humility has depressed many a genius to a hermit, but never raised one to fame.' If any Critic catches at the word *genius*, the Author tells him, once for all, that he certainly looks upon himself as possest of some poetic abilities, otherwise his publishing in the manner he has done, would be a manoeuvre below the worst character,

* Shenstone

which, he hopes, his worst enemy will ever give him: but to the genius of a Ramsay, or the glorious dawnings of the poor, unfortunate Ferguson, he, with equal uaffected sincerity, declares, that, even in his highest pulse of vanity, he has not the most distant pretensions. These two justly admired Scotch Poets he has often had in his eye in the following pieces; but rather with a view to kindle at their flame, than for servile imitation.

To his Subscribers, the Author returns his most sincere thanks. Not the mercenary bow over a counter, but the heart-throbbing gratitude of the Bard, conscious how much he is indebted to Benevolence and Friendship, for gratifying him, if he deserves it, in that dearest wish of every poetic bosom – to be distinguished. He begs his readers, particularly the Learned and the Polite, who may honor him with a perusal, that they will make every allowance for Education and Circumstances of Life: but, if after a fair, candid, and impartial criticism, he shall stand convicted of Dulness and Nonsense, let him be done by, as he would in that case do by others – let him be condemned, without mercy, to contempt and oblivion.

GLOSSARY

Words that are universally known, and those that differ from the English only by the elision of letters by apostrophes, or by varying the termination of the verb, are not inserted. The terminations may be thus known; the participle present, instead of *ing*, ends, in the Scotch Dialect, in *an* or *in*; in *an*, particularly, when the verb is composed of the participle present, and any of the tenses of the auxiliary, to be. The past time and participle past are usually made by shortening the *ed* into *'t*.

A
ABACK, behind, away
Abiegh, at a distance
Ae, one
Agley, wide of the aim
Aiver, an old horse
Aizle, a red ember
Ane, one, an
Ase, ashes
Ava, at all, of all
Awn, the beard of oats, &c.

B

BAIRAN, baring
Banie, bony
Baws'nt, having a white stripe down the face
Ben, *but and ben*, the country kitchen and parlour
Bellys, bellows
Bee, *to let bee*, to leave in quiet
Biggin, a building
Bield, shelter
Blastet, worthless
Blather, the bladder
Blink, a glance, an amorous leer, a short space of time
Blype, a shred of cloth, &c.
Boost, behoved
Brash, a sudden illness
Brat, a worn shred of Cloth
Brainge, to draw unsteadily
Braxie, a morkin sheep
Brogue, an affront
Breef, an invulnerable charm
Breastet, sprung forward
Burnewin, *q.d.* burn the wind, a Blacksmith

C

CA', to call, to drive
Caup, a small, wooden dish with two lugs, or handles
Cape stane, cope stone
Cairds, tinkers
Cairn, a loose heap of stones
Chuffie, fat-faced
Collie, a general and sometimes a particular name for country curs
Cog, or coggie, a small wooden dish without handles
Cootie, a pretty large wooden dish
Crack, conversation, to converse
Crank, a harsh, grating sound
Crankous, fretting, peevish
Croon, a hollow, continued moan
Crowl, to creep
Crouchie, crook-backed
Cranreuch, the hoar frost
Curpan, the crupper
Cummock, a short staff

D

DAUD, the noise of one falling flat, a large piece of bread, &c.

Daut, to caress, to fondle

Daimen, now and then, seldom

Daurk, a day's labour

Deleeret, delirious

Dead-sweer, very loath, averse

Dowie, crazy and dull

Donsie, unlucky, dangerous

Doylte, stupified, hebetated

Dow, am able

Dought, was able

Doyte, to go drunkenly or stupidly

Drummock, meal and water mixed raw

Drunt, pet, pettish humour

Dush, to push as a bull, ram, &c.

Duds, rags of clothes

E

EERIE, frighted; particularly the dread of spirits

Eldritch, fearful, horrid, ghastly

Eild, old age

Eydent, constant, busy

F

FA', fall, lot

Fawsont, decent, orderly

Faem, foam

Fatt'rels, ribband ends, &c.

Ferlie, a wonder, to wonder; also a term of contempt

Fecht, to fight

Fetch, to stop suddenly in the draught, and then come on too hastily

Fier, sound, healthy

Fittie lan', the near horse of the hindmost pair in the plough

Flunkies, livery servants

Fley, to frighten

Fleesh, fleece

Flisk, to fret at the yoke

Flichter, to flutter

Forbears, ancestors

Forby, besides

Forjesket, jaded
Fow, full, drunk; a bushel, &c.
Freath, froath
Fuff, to blow intermittedly
Fyle, to dirty, to soil

G

GASH, wise, sagacious, talkative; to converse
Gate, or gaet, way, manner, practice
Gab, the mouth; to speak boldly
Gawsie, jolly, large
Geck, to toss the head in pride or wantonness
Gizz, a wig
Gilpey, a young girl
Glaizie, smooth, glittering
Glunch, a frown; to frown
Glint, to peep
Grushie, of thick, stout growth
Gruntle, the visage; a grunting noise
Grousome, loathsomely grim

H

HAL, or hald, hold, hiding place
Hash, a term of contempt
Haverel, a quarter-wit
Haurl, to drag, to peel
Hain, to save, to spare
Heugh, a crag, a coal-pit
Hecht, to forebode
Histie, dry, chapt, barren
Howe, hollow
Hoste or Hoast, to cough
Howk, to dig
Hoddan, the motion of a sage country farmer on an old cart horse
Houghmagandie, a species of gender composed of the masculine and
 feminine united
Hoy, to urge incessantly
Hoyte, a motion between a trot and a gallop
Hogshouther, to justle with the shoulder

I

ICKER, an ear of corn
Ier-oe, a great grand child
Ingine, genius
Ill-willie, malicious, unkind

J

JAUK, to dally at work
Jouk, to stoop
Jocteleg, a kind of knife
Jundie, to justle

K

KAE, a daw
Ket, a hairy, ragged fleece of wool
Kiutle, to cuddle, to caress, to fondle
Kiaugh, carking anxiety
Kirsen, to christen

L

LAGGEN, the angle at the bottom of a wooden dish
Laithfu', bashful
Leeze me, a term of congratulatory endearment
Leal, loyal, true
Loot, did let
Lowe, flame; to flame
Lunt, smoke; to smoke
Limmer, a woman of easy virtue
Link, to trip along
Lyart, grey
Luggie, a small, wooden dish with one handle

M

MANTEELE, a mantle
Melvie, to soil with meal
Mense, good breeding
Mell, to meddle with
Modewurk, a mole
Moop, to nibble as a sheep
Muslin kail, broth made up simply of water, barley and greens

N

NOWTE, black cattle
Nieve, the fist

O

OWRE, over
Outler, lying in the fields, not housed at night

P

PACK, intimate, familiar
Pang, to cram
Painch, the paunch
Paughty, proud, saucy
Pattle or pettle, the plough-staff
Peghan, the crop of fowls, the stomach
Penny-wheep, small beer
Pine, pain, care
Pirratch, or porritch, pottage
Pliskie, trick
Primsie, affectedly nice
Prief, proof

Q

QUAT, quit, did quit
Quaikin, quaking

R

RAMFEEZL'D, overspent
Raep or rape, a rope
Raucle, stout, clever
Raible, to repeat by rote
Ram-stam, thoughtless
Raught, did reach
Reestet, shrivelled
Reest, to be restive
Reck, to take heed
Rede, counsel, to counsel
Ripp, a handful of unthreshed corn, &c.
Rief, reaving
Risk, to make a noise like the breaking of small roots with the plough
Rowt, to bellow

Roupet, hoarse
Runkle, a wrinkle
Rockin, a meeting on a winter evening

S

SAIR, sore
Saunt, a saint
Scrimp, scant; to stint
Scriegh, to cry shrilly
Scrieve, to run smoothly and swiftly
Screed, to tear
Scawl, a Scold
Sconner, to loath
Sheen, bright
Shaw, a little wood; to show
Shaver, a humorous mischievous wag
Skirl, a shrill cry
Sklent, to slant, to fib
Skiegh, mettlesome, fiery, proud
Slype, to fall over like a wet furrow
Smeddum, powder of any kind
Smytrie, a numerous collection of small individuals
Snick-drawing, trick-contriving
Snash, abusive language
Sowther, to cement, to solder
Splore, a ramble
Spunkie, fiery; will o' wisp
Spairge, to spurt about like water or mire, to soil
Sprittie, rushy
Squatter, to flutter in water
Staggie, diminutive of Stag
Steeve, firm
Stank, a pool of standing water
Stroan, to pour out like a spout
Stegh, to cram the belly
Stibble-rig, the reaper who takes the lead
Sten, to rear as a horse
Swith, get away
Syne, since, ago, then

T

TAPETLESS, unthinking
Tawie, that handles quietly
Tawted, or tawtet, matted together
Taet, a small quantity
Tarrow, to murmur at one's allowance
Thowless, slack, pithless
Thack an' raep, all kinds of necessaries, particularly clothes
Thowe, thaw
Tirl, to knock gently, to uncover
Toyte, to walk like old age
Trashtrie, trash

W

WAUKET, thickened as fullers do cloth
Water-kelpies, a sort of mischievous spirits that are said to haunt fords, & c.
Water-brose, brose made simply of meal and water
Wauble, to swing
Wair, to lay out, to spend
Whaizle, to wheez
Whisk, to sweep
Wintle, a wavering, swinging motion
Wiel, a small whirlpool
Winze, an oath
Wonner, wonder, a term of contempt
Wooer-bab, the garter knotted below the knee with a couple of loops and ends
Wrack, to vex, to trouble

Y

YELL, dry, spoken of a cow
Ye, is frequently used for the singular
Young-guidman, a new married man.

Appendix B

A TITLE CHANGES HANDS

Poems, Chiefly in the Scottish Dialect was to remain the title of every edition of Burns's poetry with which he had any direct connection. Significantly, he kept as the basis of the 1787 Edinburgh collection all of the poems published at Kilmarnock (only epitaphs were excluded). The 1787 volume contained in addition a group of previously unpublished poems and songs, including:

> Death and Doctor Hornbook
> The Brigs of Ayr
> The Ordination
> The Calf
> Address to the Unco Guid
> Tam Samson's Elegy
> To a Haggis
> Address to Edinburgh
> John Barleycorn
> Behind yon hills where Stinchar flows
> Green Grow the Rashes
> The gloomy night is gath'ring fast.

Whereas Burns had retained complete authorial control over his first book, he sold the copyright of the Edinburgh edition – published like its predecessor by subscription, with the poet assuming financial responsibility – to William Creech, an Edinburgh bookseller-publisher. This put Creech in a position to issue new editions for his own profit. Accordingly, in 1793 an edition in two volumes appeared under the joint imprint of William Creech and Thomas Cadell (who as Creech's London agent had handled a London edition of the 1787 *Poems*). Its principal new poem was 'Tam o' Shanter'. This edition was reissued in 1794.

Appendix C

A FINDING-LIST OF POETIC MANUSCRIPTS

Listed below are the locations of the principal recorded manuscripts of individual poems included in the Kilmarnock edition in 1786. It will be noted that two or more separate manuscripts exist for a number of poems, while other poems are known only through print. On the important manuscript collections at Irvine and Kilmarnock, see above, p. xxxii (Note on the Text). In The Centenary Edition of Burns, 1896, Henley and Henderson refer in addition to manuscripts of 'To a Mouse' and 'Epistle to Davie'; the present whereabouts of these are not known. The Huntington Library, San Marino, California, has a copy of the 1793 edition of Burns's Poems with certain minor holograph corrections. The First Commonplace Book and Adam MS are privately owned.

The Twa Dogs Irvine Burns Club; Kilmarnock Monument Museum.
Scotch Drink Irvine; Kilmarnock.
The Author's Earnest Cry and Prayer Irvine; Kilmarnock.
The Holy Fair Irvine; Kilmarnock; British Library, Egerton MS 1656.
Address to the Deil Irvine; Kilmarnock.
The Death and Dying Words of Poor Mailie Kilmarnock; First Commonplace Book.
Poor Mailie's Elegy Kilmarnock.
To J. S**** Kilmarnock.
A Dream
The Vision Burns Cottage Museum, Alloway, Stair MS.
Halloween Burns Cottage Museum, Alloway; Kilmarnock.
The Auld Farmer's New-Year-Morning Salutation Kilmarnock.
The Cotter's Saturday Night Irvine; Kilmarnock; British Library, Egerton MS 1656.
To a Mouse
Epistle to Davie Kilmarnock; Adam MS.
The Lament
Despondency

Man Was Made to Mourn Kilmarnock; First Commonplace Book.
Winter Kilmarnock; First Commonplace Book.
A Prayer in the Prospect of Death First Commonplace Book.
To a Mountain-Daisy [See note in Kinsley, p. 1173].
To Ruin
Epistle to a Young Friend Kilmarnock; Edinburgh University Library Laing
 MS.
On a Scotch Bard Gone to the West Indies Adam MS; Huntington Library,
 San Marino, California.
A Dedication to G. H. Esq
To a Louse Bodleian Library, Oxford, MS Add. A. 111.
Epistle to J. L***k** First Commonplace Book.
To the same First Commonplace Book.
To W. S***n**
To J. R******
Song, 'It was upon a Lammas night'
Song, 'Now westlin winds' First Commonplace Book; British Library, Hastie
 MS.
Song, 'From thee, Eliza, I must go'
The Farewell
A Bard's Epitaph

Appendix D

THE KILMARNOCK EDITION: A NOTE ON SECONDHAND PRICES

The centenary of Burns's birth is usually seen as the point at which copies of his first published collection began to be sought after. Enterprising individuals had anticipated this market interest; one case is recorded of someone buying a copy from an Edinburgh bookseller in the early 1850s for a shilling. By the beginning of the twentieth century, Burns had a well established saleroom reputation. Naturally, a book limited to just over 600 copies, published not in London or New York, but in a Scottish country town, has often been described as 'rare', and *Poems, Chiefly in the Scottish Dialect* (1786) has consistently been much sought after by collectors. In mint condition, with the full original margins, it *is* a scarce book, but J. C. Ewing accurately noted in the *Burns Chronicle* in 1930, 'The first edition of the *Poems* has never been "rare", though booksellers and auctioneers have long declared it to be . . .' He quotes £2,450 from a sale at Sotheby's in 1929 as 'doubtless the highest price' paid by that date. *Book Auction Records* supply recent figures broadly in keeping with this. In 1974, a copy of the book was sold by Sotheby (New York) for $9,000. Christie auctioned a Kilmarnock edition, also in New York, for $8,000 in 1981. Maggs auctioned a copy in London for £3,800 in 1979. Outside the auction room, however, copies have been known to change hands for higher prices than these.

INDEX OF FIRST LINES